GUIDE TO
LAW

ADRIAN LAING

© Haynes Publishing 2020
First published January 2020

Adrian Laing has asserted the moral right to be
identified as the author of this work.

A CIP Catalogue record for this book
is available from the British Library.

ISBN: 978 1 78521 623 7

Library of Congress control no. 2019934676

Published by Haynes Publishing,
Sparkford, Yeovil, Somerset BA22 7JJ
Tel: 01963 440635
Int. tel: +44 1963 440635
Website: www.haynes.com

Printed in Malaysia.

Bluffer's Guide®, Bluffer's® and Bluff Your Way®
are registered trademarks.

Series Editor: David Allsop.

CONTENTS

'What do you call 5,000 lawyers at the bottom of the sea? A good start.'

Anon.

A GOOD START

'I am a lawyer, therefore I know.'
'I am a bluffer-in-law, therefore others
think I know.'

All lawyers start off as bluffers-in-law; it is a necessary stage in their development and by all rights the art should remain with them when they actually *practise* being a lawyer. This book is essential to both the lawyer and the bluffer-in-law because the art of bluffing is crucial to both. There is no better bluffer than a lawyer and no better bluffer-in-law than one who comes across as a good lawyer.

And what is a 'good lawyer'? One who can give advice with the utter confidence of a seasoned bluffer: *'I think our prospects of success are quite good'* is a classic example of lawyer-speak which effectively says nothing while covering the proverbial rear with understated ambiguity. It is worthy of any modern-day google-shyster.

No professional can ever be all-knowing in their field; there is simply too much data for one person to assimilate in a single lifetime. For many professionals bluffing is not an art to assist with their day job, bluffing *is* the day job. Ask Diane Abbott or Boris Johnson, two prominent British politicians not known for having complete mastery of their briefs. Or ask Chris Grayling, Michael Gove or Liz Truss, all at some time appointed to the historic position of Lord Chancellor, one of the most senior legal offices in the land, without so much as a law degree between them.

No lawyer worth his or her salt would last a single day without being an accomplished bluffer. So many laws are passed, so often, in so many different forms and contexts, interpreted by a variety of courts and tribunals across the globe that even the highest tech voice response system could not avoid bluffer-speak if asked the question: 'But will we win?' The honest answer, most of the time, would be 'I don't know.' The bluffer knows better and would answer, confidently: 'It depends.'

Bluffing is both an art and a skill crucial to the success of any lawyer, best seen as performance art requiring total commitment to create an aura of depth and authenticity. Delivery and presentation are as important, if not more important, than content. Bluffers know this instinctively and thus every lawyer is a bluffer. Hence the best lawyers will have won you over before they speak a word because they look like lawyers. This principle applies to many professionals, whether you are a dentist or a comedian. The hard work has been done before one word is uttered. It is an art, and one which the bluffer must master.

There are of course many different types of professional legal practitioners: barristers, solicitors, legal executives, paralegals, attorneys . . . in addition to the generic term 'lawyer'. These differences are explored in some detail in this comprehensive guide, because there is a growing movement to broaden the concept of lawyers away from the conventional distinction between solicitor and barrister. The Big Idea is that the traditional legal professions should not enjoy a monopoly over the provision of legal services and that consumers are best served by finding better ways of delivering cost-effective, regulated services.

In many ways there has never been a better time to be a lawyer, but first one should learn how to bluff one's way into the wider legal profession. And that takes some time and selective study, which is what this modest work is all about: bluffing your way into the biggest bluff of all.

Therefore, focus is given to the most important aspects of what lawyers and bluffers-in-law need to know in order to provide the elusive cloak of authenticity:

a) self-belief;
b) the modern legal system in the Brexit age;
c) the regulatory context;
d) an overview of the taxonomy of law;
e) 'the politics of litigation';
f) and a touch of philosophy and literature to boot.

The Bluffer's Guide to Law seeks to provide an understanding into why so many famous people started their careers in law: from Mahatma Gandhi to Fidel Castro, John Cleese to Gerard Butler, Bob Mortimer to Clive Anderson, Margaret Thatcher to Tony Blair, to Hillary Clinton and Barack Obama. And where they go may you go too, it's just a question of mastering the art of bluffing.

And that is where this short but definitive guide comes in.* It sets out to conduct you through the main danger zones encountered in discussions about law, and to equip you with a vocabulary and evasive technique that will minimise the risk of being rumbled as a bluffer. It will give you a few easy-to-learn hints and methods that will allow you to be accepted as a legal expert of rare ability and experience. But it will do more. It will give you the tools to impress legions of marvelling listeners with your knowledge and advice – without anyone having a second thought as to whether you are a lawyer or a bluffer-in-law.

---

* Note that unless otherwise stated this *Bluffer's Guide* is concerned specifically with the legal system in England and Wales. There are separate jurisdictions in Scotland and Northern Ireland (*see* chapter 9).

TWO-LANE LEGAL HIGHWAY

The concept of a lawyer – a person who is trained and qualified to advise on the law, to draft, sign and certify legal documents, and appear before a judge in a court of law – has evolved over hundreds of years. This evolution is still very much a work in progress; soon there may be only one species left, the ultimate survivor: the 'bluffer-in-law', a person who affects to know considerably more about the law than he or she actually does.

The legal profession has seen scriveners and proctors, the serjeant-at-law, the attorney-at-law – even the high sheriff – come and go from our daily lives, but it is still essentially built around the historical fault line between barristers and solicitors. Practising barristers see themselves as advocates as of right. Traditionally solicitors are concerned with the less glamorous grind of interfacing with the public, preparing legal documentation, and generally spending more time confined to an office than to 'chambers'* or the courts.

NEVER THE TWAIN

Solicitors and barristers belong to different parts of the legal profession, sit different entry exams and practise in a completely different manner. Practising barristers think of themselves as experts from whom solicitors seek advice, upon instruction. A fully kitted-out courtroom-ready barrister would be recognised anywhere in the world as an 'advocate'. A well-dressed solicitor would be taken for a successful businessman, a badly dressed solicitor as a failed bluffer-in-law. Or 'the accused'.

However, the distinction between a solicitor and barrister representing historically separate branches of the legal profession is becoming increasingly anachronistic. There are now many barristers who practise in solicitors' firms as 'advocates' and there are many solicitors who practise in the criminal and civil courts as 'solicitor advocates'. According to a 2019 edition of the *In-House Lawyer* periodical there are an estimated 30,000 solicitors and barristers who work 'in house' in corporate roles and are called whatever the enterprise considers grandest, e.g. 'In-house Lawyer', 'Director of Legal Affairs', 'Vice-President, General Legal Counsel'. Lawyers are often

---

*Chambers are the somewhat antiquated name given by barristers and judges to their place of work. They can be in a modern office block, or in one of the four 'Inns of Court' in a place populated by other barristers and judges. 'Chambers' may also refer to the private rooms used by judges in court.

immediately placed on the board as the Company Secretary. It's like getting a bye into the final.

You must remember that in order to stay sharp and survive, you need to argue. Lawyers need disputes even if they only have themselves to argue among.

Barristers are increasingly exploring and navigating the tricky route of taking instructions (and money) directly from the 'lay' client without the involvement of solicitors. If solicitors can have rights of audience in the higher courts, then barristers – so the argument goes – should be allowed *direct access* to clients. This line of thinking has been around for many generations. You must remember that in order to stay sharp and survive, you need to argue. Lawyers need disputes even if they only have themselves to argue among.

Do say: *'Settle a case, lose a client.'*
Don't say: *'May truth and justice prevail!'*

WHO NEEDS LAWYERS?

The pertinent question for the bluffer to ask is this: do we need lawyers, or do we simply want someone trained (and preferably regulated) to do specifically what is required? If you are buying or selling a property do you go to a solicitor or a licensed conveyancer? Does the person who drafts your will need to be a 'lawyer' or a specialist in wills and probate? The consumer simply wants the job done well, on time and at a reasonable price. Why pay a senior solicitor when a junior legal executive can do the same job better, quicker and for less money?

The bluffer-in-law should take great comfort in the fact that recent governments do not seem to like barristers, or solicitors. The Legal Services Board (LSB) now grants permission for specific legal activities to be undertaken by authorised individuals and sits very much above the organisations which actively regulate solicitors and barristers. (These regulatory bodies are considered in a later chapter.) The most recent significant legislative turning point in the evolution of the lawyer was the passing of the Legal Services Act 2007, which side-steps where possible references to barristers or solicitors and focuses instead on what lawyers are, or are not, allowed to do. So, if you are inclined to pore over the 2007 Act pay attention to the idea of *reserved legal activities*' and put aside any preconception that a lawyer has to be either a solicitor or a barrister.

The 2007 Act (Part 5) created a new legal entity – Alternative Business Structures (ABS). This allows lawyers to practise in a way that most other English-speaking jurisdictions understand – a legal profession which is not actually 'fused' but at least appears that way, by permitting lawyers not only to work together but alongside other professionals such as accountants. But not estate agents (unless you happen to be in Scotland, where they do things differently).

A CHANGING LANDSCAPE

In 2014, Chris Grayling, the then Bluffer-in-Chief (*see* Glossary) exercised his power as Lord Chancellor under the 2007 Legal Services Act, designating the Chartered Institute of Legal Executives (CILEx) as a licensing body for reserved legal activities including rights of audience, conduct of litigation and 'reserved activities' in the fields of probate and conveyancing. These developments have the same aim – to allow a person who has not qualified as a solicitor or barrister to fulfil a task which previously could only be undertaken by (guess who) a solicitor or barrister. In a different era, when the 'senior' branches of the profession had a virtual monopoly on the provision of legal services, this would have been unthinkable. The bluffer-in-law can therefore afford to take the line that the changing legal landscape can only be a force for good for the consumer, but not necessarily for those who thought they had a divine and exclusive right to represent a client in court or prepare legal documentation.

GREAT BALLS OF FIRE

The bluffer-in-law should already be sniffing great opportunities ahead because the current narrative as expressed in the CILEx application to the LSB is bluffer-speak of the highest order:

We believe that greater diversity of opportunity within the legal market can assist in developing consumer choice and better ways to deliver better services.

This speaks to the 2007 Act in its own language; preying on the idea of consumer choice and 'greater diversity'. This is great news for bluffers, not so good for barristers and solicitors who look up to the sky with the innocent expression of a complacent dinosaur: 'I wonder if that asteroid has got anything to do with me?' And that ball of flame has a name: it is called 'The PD-GAT', otherwise known as 'the public don't give a toss'.

There are now many entry points into Lawyer Land because the legally recognised approach road, a modest dual carriageway – solicitors to the left and barristers to the right – has been greatly broadened into a super highway and now warmly embraces legal executives, licensed conveyancers, commissioners for oaths, patent and trademark attorneys, immigration advisers, paralegals and legal 'assistants' among many others (addressed later). There will also be closer scrutiny of the ways to qualify and practise as a lawyer, including the lesser known species of the 'notary public' and the 'cost draftsman'.

The distinction between lawyers, solicitors and barristers has had its time, the game is up, the writing is on the wall; it is an analogue bifurcation in a digital world. The future is for lawyers, bluffers one and all.

In the following pages aspiring bluffers will tiptoe their way through the different powers and functions of the Legal Services Board, the Law Society, the Solicitors' Regulation Authority, the Bar Council and the Bar Standards Board. And where does the Legal Ombudsman fit in? A rudimentary understanding of the *regulatory* system of lawyers will allow you to out-bluff most lawyers on the subject of regulation because they are now just so *weary* of the increasingly burdensome and expensive regulatory environment. The distinction between lawyers, solicitors and barristers has had its time, the game is up, the writing is on the wall; it is an analogue bifurcation in a digital world. The future is for lawyers, bluffers one and all.

A FRIEND CALLED MAC

A word or two about the much maligned and unfairly ridiculed, self-confessed bluffer-in-law known as the 'McKenzie Friend' – the non-trained 'adviser' who provides 'reasonable assistance' to a person in court who for whatever reason is without formal legal representation.

This practice was judicially recognised in the family courts as far back as 1970 but few judges will allow a McKenzie Friend to address the court, especially if they look as if they might know what they are talking about. A true McKenzie Friend is likely to have been up for days researching the law and mastering the detail of the case because he or she cares about the effect the outcome of the hearing will have on their friend. However, an individual who seeks to make a quick buck out of pretending to be a 'friend' and thinks they can charge good money to act as an 'advocate' without any training or emotional attachment to the case is not a friend, McKenzie or otherwise. These people are shysters and give bluffers a bad name.

AUDIENCE PARTICIPATION

A 'right of audience' was traditionally a heavily protected prerogative of barristers – those called to one of the four Inns of Court: Inner Temple, Middle Temple, Gray's Inn and Lincoln's Inn. Judges, mostly of barristerial stock (more of that later), prefer to be addressed in court by fellow barristers who tend to speak in that tone of voice associated with a private education. It's all about *form*, dear boy.

But what if a bluffer-in-law defended himself and fared as well as, if not performed better than, his barrister or solicitor opponent? What if the professional lost to the amateur? It does happen – so-called 'litigants in person' do sometimes win but that can be excused on the basis that the case 'turned on its facts', nothing to do with an amateur bettering a professional on a point of law, nor simply one bluffer out-bluffing another. No, of course not. That would be unthinkable.

A true bluffer-in-law should be able to articulate with confidence and in one breath, a coherent statement demonstrating with consummate ease and effortless authority an understanding of the world of 'lawyers'.

OLD SCHOOL

Bluffing is one matter, misleading the public is another. If you 'mistakenly' hold yourself out as a qualified lawyer the consequences can be draconian – because you are holding yourself out to be what you are not, and that can land you in what is technically known as 'ordure'. What the bluffer-in-law will now know is that the legal landscape is changing very quickly. Until recently the traditional concept of a 'lawyer' embraced barristers and solicitors who fought among themselves over rights of audience and direct access to clients. In the meantime, the world around them changed and a new species of lawyer evolved. There is now an 'old school' of solicitors and barristers and a 'new school' of professional legal practitioners who are entitled to call themselves 'lawyers'. Somewhere among the old and new is the bluffer-in-law.

To master the subtle distinction between a bluffer-in-law and a *qualified* lawyer involves gingerly dipping a toe into the world of exams and qualifications even if the purpose of the enquiry is knowing what to avoid. Know enough about the examination route to becoming a lawyer and people might reasonably assume that you have travelled it. First, you will need to know that the qualification process varies enormously depending on what type of lawyer you are aiming to be, or not to be; that is the question.

BARRISTERS

> 'I often think that knowledge of the law is a bit of a handicap to a barrister.'
>
> *Rumpole of the Bailey*

The Bar Standards Board (BSB) set out in detail the routes to qualifying as a barrister. First, it is important to distinguish between a 'qualified barrister' and a 'practising barrister'. To call yourself a practising barrister you must have an annually granted practising certificate from the Bar Council. You will have obtained a good undergraduate degree (at the very least a 2.2). If that degree was in law – what the BSB calls a QLD (qualifying law degree) – you're then straight into the Bar finals, a one-year course (via the BCAT, *see* below). If your degree was not in law, then you'll need to pass another exam (a conversion course) to sit the Bar exams. These conversion qualifications are of two types but serve the purpose of ensuring you have a foundation in law: the Common Professional

Examination (CPE) or an approved Graduate Diploma in Law (GDL) course. The Bar Professional Training Course (BPTC) – the 'Bar exams' – are thought of as very easy by some and almost impossible by others. This is because you are being tested for your suitability to qualify as a barrister. The powers that be already know you can bluff your way through a written exam. If you approach the BPTC simply as a test of your academic brilliance you are heading for a very painful fall. They want to know that you can think and advise as a barrister; in a 'real' way, forensically and practically. For example, an intermediate step required between the academic stage and the BPTC is a test called the Bar Course Aptitude Test (BCAT), which addresses the would-be barrister's 'critical thinking and reasoning' but does not test legal knowledge. Some get it, others fail and go through life never understanding how they can be so smart and yet fail an 'easy' set of exams. If in doubt, find the money and pay a good tutor to explain it to you. That's on top of the fees for the BPTC itself which will vary from around £12,000 to £19,000 depending on which one of the eight BSB authorised courses you decide to roll the dice with. These entry costs are increasing year on year, as is the cost of living whether the course is based in London, Leeds, Bristol, Nottingham or Cardiff. So research into the real, total costs involved and the relative success rates of each of the courses is well advised. So, you pass the BPTC, and you may now be 'called to the Bar'. You've gone through all the hoops and loops of the academic stage, the aptitude test and the finals, and therefore you are ready to be 'called to the Bar' without further ado, surely? Not quite. What does being 'called' actually mean? It means what it says, of course. You must wait your turn in an ill-fitting gown and literally be called to the Bar in one of the four Inns of Court. The student approaches 'the Bar' (i.e. a high table), exchanges a few disorderly and unrehearsed nods and bows, retreats red-faced and is instantly transformed into a 'barrister'. It's enough to give bluffers-in-law a bad name.

But the Inns must keep up their traditions otherwise they might forget what they are for, so the would-be barrister must also complete 12 'qualifying sessions' (or qualifying 'units') helpfully defined by the BSB as 'educational and collegiate activities arranged by or on behalf of the Inn(s) for the purpose of preparing BPTC students for practice'.

In times past this meant attending your Inn for at least 12 dinners to sit with experienced 'real' barristers and by some form of port-induced osmosis acquire the knowledge of the ages from 'senior practitioners'. However, being the progressive bodies that they are the Inns have modified the concept of 'dining' to include 'networking and development opportunities' such as training workshops, talks and weekend courses.

Once called you are entitled to describe yourself as a qualified barrister, and can now wear a theatrical hairpiece, a black gown, and a fresh supply of detachable 'stiff' winged collars and starched flappy 'bands'. If you've bluffed this far, you might well be feeling rather pleased with yourself. But you're still not going to get that practising certificate just yet because there's another hurdle to overcome: pupillage, which is one year of practical training under the wing of a pupil master.

Getting him or her on side, usually by unpaid stints of writing their 'counsel's opinions' (a process you will come to know as 'devilling') is vital, because your pupil master will have a big say in how your career progresses.

Traditionally pupillage is split into the 'first six months' and the 'second six'. Only after the first six can a barrister (though still a 'pupil' barrister) take on a case on their own. After completion of the second six the pupil is entitled to obtain a practising certificate and hold themselves out as a practising barrister.

As a rough guide there is a 50/50 chance of being 'taken on' from pupil to tenant although that is probably a generous estimate. It is like a year-long interview and many small chambers effectively operate a black ball system; alienate one member of chambers and you're clean bowled.

However, you still need to find somewhere to practise from – and that is the biggest filter of all. Of all those called to the Bar in any one year maybe 25% will get a 'tenancy' (a 'place' in a 'set' of chambers). The sensible 75% take their certificate and look for a real job with regular pay, and even a pension.

For example, the BSB states that in the year

2017/2018, 1,351 graduates were called to the Bar. In the same year 313 new tenancies were awarded. Not everyone called to the Bar enters pupillage and chambers are acutely aware of the expectations a pupillage creates. The numbers of tenancies awarded each year can vary with each set of chambers. If there are four pupils in a medium-sized 'set' they might take on one, or two. But not four. As a rough guide there is a 50/50 chance of being 'taken on' from pupil to tenant although that is probably a generous estimate. It is like a year-long interview and many small chambers effectively operate a black ball system; alienate one member of chambers and you're clean bowled.

The BSB has, thoughtfully, posted a 'health warning' to would-be barristers. It should be read with great care. It can be paraphrased as follows:

> *The Bar can offer an extremely rewarding career if you: have a high level of intellectual ability; are highly articulate in written and spoken English; can think and communicate under pressure and have determination and stamina, and are emotionally robust.*

The bluffer should take heart from this warning. They aren't asking for much, really. To be a barrister you must be smart, be able to read and write well, not crack under pressure and be determined. The 'emotionally robust' element is interesting and should be taken as a subtle means of warding away people who can't take being humiliated in court by an impatient judge or a more experienced opponent. It also means – in the context of the criminal Bar – that you will be obliged to defend rapists, robbers and murderers. If that thought turns your stomach, perhaps the Bar isn't quite your cup of tea.

However, if you stay the course, after 15 years or so you may feel confident enough to apply (and pay over £3K) to 'take silk' – the right to wear a silk gown in court, otherwise known as being appointed a Queen's Counsel. About 200 or so applications are made every year, predominantly from the list of practising barristers. According to the BSB there were 1,695 QCs at the Bar of England and Wales in 2018 and a further 108 appointed in 2019. This recognition of your exalted status is a significant badge of honour and can have a dramatic effect on earning power. The system is far more open than in times past but only a handful of solicitors and those who make a significant contribution to the law outside a legal practice can expect to be granted the privilege. For some members of the Bar not to be awarded silk is a sad day indeed. Terribly sad. But, keep your hopes up and apply next year – you never know.

SOLICITORS

'Should I qualify as a solicitor or a barrister?' That question has been asked countless times by student bluffers-in-law conditioned to believe there are only two routes to becoming a 'lawyer'. Nonetheless, the most frequent answer (by a long margin) is solicitor. The bluffer-in-law, perhaps cautious of even asking the question, should know why there are so many more solicitors than barristers. As with barristers, there are three principal stages to qualifying as a solicitor:

1. obtain a degree (although there is no minimum 2:2 honours requirement as there is at the Bar);
2. sit the Legal Practice Course (LPC) which is a compulsory entry point. As with barristers if your first degree is not in law then the candidate will need to sit a recognised Graduate Diploma in Law course. Life can be so unfair;
3. complete two years post-qualification training.

At first sight the solicitor route takes longer because barristers need only complete one year of pupillage whereas solicitors need to complete two years' training. The difference is that trainee solicitors get paid a salary from the moment they sign up, earning the sort of income (with benefits) that the majority of pupil barristers can only dream of.

The other reason why so many more would-be lawyers qualify as solicitors as opposed to barristers is primarily because there are far fewer chambers to practise from than there are firms of solicitors.

According to the BSB in 2018, there were less than 413 chambers and 16,598 barristers with practising certificates. By comparison, the Annual Statistics Report of the Law Society states that as at July 2019, there were 146,913 solicitors with practising certificates. That vast army of solicitors practise from 10,385 'firms', which range from one-man bands (there are over 2,000 'sole practitioners') to mega-firms based in the USA with offices all over the world.

The key term in solicitor-world is not lawyer but 'fee-earner'. You are what you earn, and it's hard to bluff otherwise; here money talks and power in these circles is determined by your contacts, client base and your bottom line.

Bluffers take note: Baker & McKenzie is ranked as the world's top law firm in terms of revenue, markets and international lawyer count. The *Financial Times* reported in April 2019 that it had over 4,700 employees with a global turnover of $2.96bn and operates in nearly 50 countries. The largest set of chambers in the UK (by number of barristers), is 'No 5 Chambers' which has over 250 barristers, with offices in London, Birmingham, Bristol and Leicester.

The key term in solicitor-world is not lawyer but 'fee-earner'. You are what you earn, and it's hard to bluff otherwise; here money talks and power in these circles is determined by your contacts, client base and your bottom line.

It is still the case that members of the Bar are perceived as being far more elitist than their counterparts in the Law Society. Commercially orientated companies tend to view solicitors as more connected to the 'real world' than members of the Bar. Furthermore, solicitors are far less inhibited about personally negotiating fees with clients and not delegating such 'delicate' matters to an agent, otherwise known as the barrister's clerk.

However, the numbers will tell you that your chances of being made a judge – of one type or another – are greatly improved if you apply from the Bar, which is still seen as the traditional route to 'the bench'. Relatively few solicitors see this as a career objective anyway, despite the lucrative public sector pension.

There is also the historic perception of members of the Bar as day-to-day advocates, a very specialist occupation requiring highly developed forensic skills. And it shouldn't be forgotten that practising barristers are self-employed. Some make a mint; others struggle financially throughout their entire career. It's a high-risk strategy.

It is a safer route to qualify and practise as a solicitor; the rewards can be as great if not greater than those enjoyed by a successful barrister. A newly qualified solicitor is likely to earn more money far more quickly than a junior at the Bar. Although the public's perception of barristers is one of guaranteed riches, it can take many years before a barrister is earning an above-average salary on a regular basis.

NEW SCHOOL

LEGAL EXECUTIVES

Qualifying as a 'Chartered Legal Executive' (CLE) is becoming an increasingly popular route to practising law, as a recognised lawyer in direct competition with barristers and solicitors. According to the website of the Chartered Institute of Legal Executives (CILEx) there are now well over 20,000 'chartered legal executive lawyers'. There is no doubt that CLEs are on the march; they tend to specialise and work for solicitors, but they are becoming increasingly independent and are establishing a network of stand-alone legal advisory services.

The main appeal of qualifying through CILEx is that it is not quite so precious about entry point qualifications. In fact, it recommends that you have a minimum of '4 GCSEs grade C or above including English Language or Literature'. In other words, it will view your application on its own merits and decide according to your personal circumstances.

CILEx is also far more accommodating about the time it might take to qualify – there is no time limit and therefore you may progress in accordance with how your life permits you to devote your time, energy and money towards qualification. This is eminently sensible. However, you must work under the supervision of a lawyer (by which they mean a solicitor, barrister, CLE or licensed conveyancer) for a recommended period of three years.

There is no doubt that CLEs are on the march; they tend to specialise and work for solicitors, but they are becoming increasingly independent and are establishing a network of stand-alone legal advisory services.

The regulated legal executive appears at first glance to be one of the newest lawyer-species but, in fact, it is one of the oldest. This is because its evolution is based not on academic ability, but on the idea of an apprenticeship, namely, learning on the job. Becoming a CLE can take much longer than qualifying as a barrister or solicitor, but it is arguably a better route to becoming a lawyer because the rite of passage is based on experience, not the ability to pass exams.

LICENSED CONVEYANCERS

Licensed conveyancers, as regulated specialists in both property and probate law have been recognised since 1985. They are regulated by the Council for Licensed Conveyancers (CLC) and to practise as such you need to pass the CLC exams.

As with legal executives there is no need to have a degree to start the course (which comprises six levels) but a degree will of course entitle you to start higher up the ladder.

LCs are regulated by the CLC, so to call yourself a LC you need to join the CLC. This process of *'rights through membership'* is common around much of the English-speaking world (especially southern hemisphere Commonwealth countries) and explains a great deal about how jurisdictions license specific activities – you join a 'club', abide by their rules and guidelines, pay your subscription and display their framed certificate in your office. Simple really.

COMMISSIONERS FOR OATHS

Even some lawyers have difficulty in distinguishing between a 'witness statement' and an 'affidavit' or 'sworn statement'. You'll know the difference when it hits.

A modern witness statement is simply a *statement of fact* using precise wording required for its use, for example in court. You declare the content to be true and sign it. An affidavit or sworn statement is needed when the circumstances specifically demand an 'oath' to be part of the statement. Although the distinction is becoming less of an issue, it does apply when, for example, there is an international element to the statement and the other jurisdiction requires the statement to be taken under oath.

Solicitors, legal executives and licensed conveyancers are automatically deemed to be commissioners for oaths, as are barristers – provided they have a practising certificate.

NOTARY PUBLIC

The Notaries Society explains: *'Notaries are primarily concerned with the authentication and certification of signatures, authority and capacity relating to documents for use abroad.'*

Is there a difference between a notary public and a commissioner for oaths? Is there a difference between a cane and walking stick? Yes, but does the bluffer care? No. Why? Because there are less than 800 'official' notaries according to the Notaries Society and they only see sunlight when a document or signature needs to be authenticated for overseas jurisdictions, providing of course that such jurisdiction does not treat other 'lawyers' (e.g. solicitors, barristers, legal executives and licensed conveyancers) as having the right to perform the same function. But as a niche profession, don't knock it – particularly if you have a second language in your CV war chest.

PATENT AND TRADEMARK ATTORNEYS

In Dickens's time the term 'attorney' was in widespread use for a lawyer who practised in the common law courts, whereas solicitors (who always thought of themselves as a cut above 'mere' attorneys) practised in the Chancery courts. By the end of the 19th century 'attorneys' had all but disappeared but a trademark or patent attorney is certainly a 'lawyer', always has been.

Parliament still has an 'Attorney-General', the term 'Lasting Power of Attorney' is now part of the legal vernacular (in the context of 'attorneys' appointed to protect the interests of people who lack the mental capacity to make decisions for themselves), and the term 'attorney' has stuck with those lawyers specialising in trademarks and patents. The term has also travelled widely, particularly to the USA where the term 'attorney-at-law' is probably more commonly used than 'lawyer'.

To qualify as a trademark or patent attorney carries significant professional respect among the wider legal fraternity because anyone who engages with intellectual property understands how valuable their technical knowledge and experience can be, particularly in the process of applying for and being granted a trade-mark or patent. There are many ways to qualify as either a trademark or a patent attorney and the route to qualification depends on your entry point. A law degree helps but is not essential.

There are three bodies to know about: the Chartered Institute of Patent Attorneys (CIPA); the Chartered Institute of Trade Mark Attorneys (CITMA) and the

Intellectual Property Regulation Board (IPReg), which regulates 'the entry route, codes of professional conduct and a complaints structure' for members of the CITMA and CIPA.

The CIPA is the professional and examining body for patent attorneys in the United Kingdom. The Institute was founded in 1882 and was incorporated by Royal Charter in 1891. It represents over 2,000 chartered patent attorneys who practise in industry and in private practice. Their total membership is over 3,500 and includes trainee patent attorneys and 'other professionals with an interest in intellectual property matters'. The CITMA is a professional membership organisation for over 1,500 registered trademark professionals; founded in 1934 it was granted its Charter in 2016.

IMMIGRATION LAWYERS / ADVISERS

In 1999, the Labour government passed the Immigration and Asylum Act in response to criticisms that the Labour Party was 'soft' on immigration.

For the bluffer to understand 'legal advice' in the context of the politically charged arena of immigration, note should be taken of the not-so-friendly advice on the government website concerning 'immigration advisers':

It is a criminal offence for a person to provide immigration advice or services in the UK unless their organisation is regulated by the Office of the Immigration Services Commissioner (OISC) or is otherwise covered by the Immigration and Asylum Act 1999. Members of certain professional bodies may give immigration advice without registering with OISC.

'Members of certain professional bodies' include – as the bluffer would now expect – barristers, solicitors and chartered legal executives.

This is regulation at its most muddled. The word 'lawyer' is avoided by the regulator but not by the public. Would a consumer ever question an immigration adviser who called themselves a 'lawyer'? They advise on the law, and to the consumer they are more than a lawyer; they are *experts in immigration*. There is a whole industry of advisers meeting a consumer demand for specialist immigration advice, and who are therefore 'lawyers' whether they are recognised as such, or not.

And if you want to hold the title of 'qualified immigration adviser' it is best to read up on the guidelines issued by the OISC. No entry exams are specified; the critical issue is one of competence, as judged by the OISC:

An individual or organisation will be considered competent to provide immigration advice or services if they can sufficiently demonstrate to the commissioner the necessary knowledge and skills required to meet the needs of clients seeking immigration advice or services at a specified advice level and category. This includes an organisation's capability to act competently in the manner in which it operates its business.

COSTS DRAFTSMAN / LAWYER

The Association of Costs Lawyers should be acknowledged in this context not least because the 'costs draftsman', who specialises in the assessment of legal costs, has recently been renamed a costs 'lawyer'. Costs lawyers may be granted rights of audience, acting as commissioners for oaths and conducting litigation. The Costs Lawyer Standards Board (CLSB) awards the practising certificate after completion of a three-year 'modular' training course. In addition costs lawyers are required to have spent at least five years working in this field.

COMPANY SECRETARY

A position as a full-time company secretary can be a lucrative but exacting task.

If the business has evolved into a complex international network of companies and subsidiaries a tax savvy 'Group Company Secretary' is likely to be very well paid indeed.

There is no reason why a company secretary cannot be called 'Company Secretary and Lawyer'. Here it is not about bluffing but knowing the nitty-gritty of what must be done, and when.

There are fundamental differences between private companies and a company which has issued shares to the public. There is no legal requirement for a company secretary of a private company to be a lawyer of any description. In fact, there is no legal requirement for a private company even to have a company secretary, at all. But the rules are stricter for *public* companies. If the company is 'public', it must appoint a company secretary who meets legal standards under the Companies Act which means either being a solicitor, barrister or member of a recognised organisation such as the Institute of Chartered Secretaries and Administrators (ICSA), which is a professional organisation in its own right.

The lesson to bluffers is this: a legally registered company will need a 'secretary' whether a legal requirement or not. Papers need to be circulated, important and timely announcements made, documents registered with Companies House. Legal formalities understood, precisely. There is no reason why a company secretary cannot be called 'Company Secretary and Lawyer'. Here it is not about bluffing but knowing the nitty-gritty of what must be done, and when.

If in doubt, ask Companies House.

PARALEGALS

The National Association of Paralegals (NAP) provides an important service to lawyers because by creating a service industry to the legal profession it enhances the reputation and status of a formally qualified legal assistant (much like a 'paramedic' and a doctor of medicine.)

Paralegals are invariably and unfairly viewed as being not just junior to but *inferior* to 'real' lawyers. As if a mechanic is lesser than a driver. Working irregular and unsocial hours as a freelance paralegal can be a real opportunity to earn good money, get a foot in the door, gain invaluable experience and keep alive hopes of earning the rewards of being a 'full status' legal professional. It is not so much that knowledge is power; it's that the *appearance of knowledge* is power (the mantra of bluffers everywhere). Lawyers beware, there is no better bluffer-in-law-in-waiting than a keen paralegal. Paralegals may be treated as if they are at the bottom of the legal food-chain, but they are doing the slog, the real hard graft and in time that experience will be rewarded.

Is a paralegal a 'lawyer'? The bluffer-in-law already knows the answer to that one: *'It depends.'* If a response, in its context, is giving the impression that the paralegal is a qualified solicitor, barrister or chartered legal executive, the answer should be: 'No, I'm a paralegal.'

In many firms of solicitors paralegals are, in reality, 'fee earners' and may understandably consider that the answer to the question could be: *'Depends how you define lawyer, I suppose.'* But here the ice is getting thin. Chances are what the client really wants to know is: 'Can you do the job and how much do you charge?'

THE REAL BIT

The ability and determination to get through years of law exams is not the whole story. It is one thing to bluff one's way into law by mastering the technique of passing exams; it is quite another getting away with it – for real.

Lawyers argue, calmly and rationally, and the bluffer-in-law must follow suit. Losing one's rag, or 'venting' as it is sometimes called, is very easy. You open your mouth, press the 'I don't care about the consequences' button and let rip. Lawyers don't vent, they argue cogently. In a courtroom, boardroom, Skype or telephone call, or during an email exchange, it is the lawyer who is expected to maintain an air of professional calmness. Expressing genuine emotion is the antithesis of bluffing. It's not about being emotionally 'robust'; it's about being emotionally intelligent.

A lawyer must also look and sound the part. This is crucial to the bluffer-in-law. It is the *'appearance'* of knowledge that matters – and this is a skill known to all bluffers; lawyers have no monopoly on this one, as any politician (or television presenter) will tell you. Self-belief is all, otherwise known as confidence.

Losing one's rag, or 'venting' as it is sometimes called, is very easy. You open your mouth, press the 'I don't care about the consequences' button and let rip. Lawyers don't vent, they argue cogently.

CONFIDENCE AND PUBLIC SPEAKING

It should now be clear to the bluffer-in-law that there are numerous ways to practise (legally and honestly) as a lawyer without the years of slog. But be careful what you wish for. You could well end up on the board of a private company being asked to read out a statement to the company's shareholders, or make a detailed presentation, or make a judgement as to whether a threat of legal action is a bluff or very real. Your GCSE in law, combined with your passionate interest and knowledge in legal matters may well have created the unchallenged aura of a 'lawyer' but a bluffer must not only be prepared to walk the walk but to talk the talk.

All law-related bluffing will end abruptly if you have not mastered the art of speaking confidently in public. Some are natural orators while others will never, ever conquer their nerves. Most people are terrified of public speaking and quite rightly so. There is a lot at stake. Whether it's a best man's speech or addressing a jury, disaster awaits like a cruel shadow intent on enveloping and crushing its victim at the first sign of weakness. It's painful to watch and humiliating to experience. A full-scale meltdown can end a career, and second chances are rarely given (or successful).

Trying to *tell* someone how to speak well in public is as effective as suggesting to someone who is overweight to eat less and exercise more. Or admonishing a smoker or alcoholic with the line – 'just give it up'. Telling a person before an important speech: 'Just relax, you'll be fine' isn't going to help. They are either ready or they are not.

Here's the key to delivering a good speech: be honest with yourself and practise. A bad singer can practise all they want and will still sing badly. But a person lacking in confidence who records and listens critically to their talk, rehearses again and again, will eventually notice a real improvement because it really is a matter of self-belief. And remember to breathe; forget that one and you'll wake up looking at a crowd of concerned people asking: 'Are you OK?'

INTERVIEWS

It is tempting to give glib advice to job interviewees – 'Be yourself, stay confident – you'll be all right.' No, you won't. They are not looking for you, they are looking for someone who can do the job and who will fit in. That person might be you, but the odds are not in your favour.

So, for the bluffer-in-law, in the context of the interview for the promising position of let's say 'junior lawyer – with prospects' here's some do-or-die advice:

- Look like a lawyer: smart, well groomed, alert.
- Shake hands like a lawyer. The handshake should be firm (but not too tight or lingering) – and a proper *grip* not a token, moist, limp affair.
- Prepare like a lawyer: you've researched the company, you understand the skill-sets required. You're a professional in the making, a bluffer putting your best foot forward.
- Speak like a lawyer: don't be afraid of a little pause – you are engaging your brain – slow down, look at the person you are speaking to. A winning smile helps.
- Listen like a lawyer: a lawyer listens inquisitively and with great interest. Practise your best 'earnest look'.
- Try saying 'I don't know.' This is the true bluffer's bluff. Of course, if the question is 'Why do you want this job?' or 'Which school did you go to?' and you say 'I don't know', expect that to be the last question you're asked before being escorted off the premises by security.
- Think of any excuse to say – at the best point in time and whether you are asked or not – why you are the best person for the job. And mean it.
- Never say: 'I need the money' when asked why you want the job. Or, 'I owe my dealer.' They want a competent bluffer, not a person who speaks 'truths that may never be spoken'.

- Never be late; better one hour early than two minutes late. Find the nearest café. Chill.
- Your social media profile confirms that you are a sane and sober lawyer in the making.

Of course, if the question is 'Why do you want this job?' or 'Which school did you go to?' and you say 'I don't know', expect that to be the last question you're asked before being escorted off the premises by security.

WHAT IS 'EFFECTIVE COMMUNICATION'?

Confidence – or 'over-confidence' – can be a burden and can lull the bluffer into confusing confidence with a completely different skill, which is *engaging* the audience. With a jury you are treated like a comedian at open-mic night. If they don't like you, they fall asleep muttering very unflattering remarks such as 'Will this torture never end?' Just carry on and try a different tack. Smile, like a bluffer on an unpaid-for sunbed.

To be effective in communication is skill and art in equal measure. Never talk down to an audience, nor patronise them. Treat them with respect but be prepared to challenge them. The worst crime is to be boring, that is unforgivable. The best tip to be effective is to do as much homework as you can fit in, not just on your subject but on your audience. Above all understand the time constraints, most often less is more.

Rehearse, of course – but not to the point of losing any sense of spontaneity. A few notes giving guidance to ensure you do not lose your thread is far more engaging than reading a script. When you feel ready, try giving a talk with no notes at all. Use PowerPoint if that's what the audience expects and wants, but don't overdo the number of slides and remember that eye contact is as important with a large group as with a single individual. Just connect with the audience; it is the most engaging form of communication – the audience will respect your courage the fewer props you have to lean on. Remember the holy trinity of public speaking: the very beginning, the middle and the route to the exit. It's like an aeroplane flight: take off, cruise, land.

THE POINT OF QUALIFICATION

There was a time, long gone, when a university law degree would automatically secure the graduate a well-paid job; if not in law then perhaps in journalism, industry, the civil service or banking.

The downside of encouraging as many students as possible to broaden their minds, increase their skills-set and obtain a degree is that the market is saturated with highly qualified, able candidates.

Many would-be lawyers (of the old school type) simply can't find a training contract to make effective use of their solicitor qualifications, nor can would-be barristers secure pupillage in a very small number of chambers with no room for new 'tenants'.

But make no mistake, the rewards for those determined, lucky or persistent enough are spectacular. The legal route is far more competitive than in the past, simply due to the imbalance of supply and demand. To put it bluntly there are too many lawyers around.

The commercial side of education is a brutal game, governed by the law of survival, otherwise known as 'Darwin got it right first time.'

According to *Social Trends 40*, the 40th anniversary edition of the annual social report last published in 2010 by the Office for National Statistics, in the academic year 1970/71 there were 621,000 students in higher education in the UK. The research body 'Universities UK' states that in the academic year 2016 /17 there were 2.32 million. There are now 163 institutions offering higher education courses. Courses compete for students, and those that don't succeed in attracting enough numbers go to the wall. The commercial side of education is a brutal game, governed by the law of survival, otherwise known as 'Darwin got it right first time.'

The consequences for those with a law degree, or even those who go one or two steps further down the training route, are that the rewards – initially at least – are far removed from the days of old. The Institute for Fiscal Studies published a detailed study in June 2018 analysing 'the relative labour market returns to different degrees'. Of the 30 subjects on the list, law came 12th, behind politics and not far ahead of geography and philosophy. The top three subjects were medicine, economics and mathematics.

But here's the rub: bluffers-in-law don't want to be doctors or deal with numbers, data and complex mathematical algorithms unless they are challenging the payment due for their mobile phone. The bluffer-in-law wants to be seen as a lawyer, a good one, and preferably well paid.

That said, in terms of routes to the top there's no doubt that a first-class degree from a good university – irrespective of the subject matter – will enhance your earning capacity considerably. Several studies were analysed by the *Guardian* in 2016 and found unequivocally that those graduates with a 'Desmond' (2:2) earn less than those with an 'Attila' (2:1) and if blessed with a 'Geoff Hurst' (1st) the prospects were even brighter. If burdened with a 'Douglas Hurd' (3rd), then read this work carefully, you'll need extra special skill in bluffing your way up the greasy pole because you will be fighting intellectual snobbery your entire life.

You will need to demonstrate that your third-class degree is totally irrelevant to your hidden potential and natural ability, as did David Dimbleby, Hugh Laurie, Carol Vorderman, A.A. Milne and the polemicist Christopher Hitchens (one of the most respected intellectuals of his day). You will need a miracle to get a decent training contract with a 3rd and the Bar has now decided that there's no point in even applying to enrol on its conversion degree and training course. You will have to prove them wrong the hard way, by perseverance and self-belief that you are not defined, for the rest of your life, by the class of your degree.

If burdened with a 'Douglas Hurd' (3rd), then read this work carefully, you'll need extra special skill in bluffing your way up the greasy pole because you will be fighting intellectual snobbery your entire life.

So, what is important to many but by no means to all employers is not just the subject matter of the degree but its class. Therefore the presumption must be that a 1st in humanities, for example, would be a better bet than a 2:1 in law, and that's an argument that any self-respecting bluffer can make.

However, bluffers should be beware. This general rule is subject to exceptions and these exceptions matter. Some barristers' chambers are particularly precious about their members triumphantly waving firsts (preferably double-firsts), and fluency in a second language to boot (preferably in Chinese, Russian or German). But many firms of solicitors have different preferences and it would be both dangerous and naive to think that any 1st will trump any other degree. Or, for example, that a 2:2 from an Oxbridge college may have more cachet than a 1st from a 'new' university. But again, be careful – the 'birds of a feather' principle (aka nepotism) is alive and well and still very much thriving in the legal world. And that principle goes way back – to your 'prep' school and your secondary school. And the profession of your parents, and so on. Institutions which have been in existence for literally hundreds of years survive by their ability to resist change and to perpetuate the old order. The real trick is to understand where your degree is most valued.

SHOW ME THE MONEY

A question a bluffer would never ask is: 'How much do lawyers earn?' because it betrays a total ignorance about how many different types of lawyers there are, and what they do.

It is like asking 'How much does a professional footballer earn?' The question would need to be more specific.

Some lawyers earn less than the minimum wage, others earn about the same as a busy scaffolder in Hastings at about £22 per hour, others are earning a modest wage in the region of £35–£50K p.a., even less earning more than £100,000 p.a. and a few – a very few – earning literally millions (of pounds, sterling) every year.

As a rule, the biggest fees are paid to specialist QCs in finance and property who can command fees of more than £1,000 per hour for out-of-court advisory work. If you want to book an in-form QC for a five-day commercial law trial, then be prepared to pay whatever fee their senior clerk considers 'appropriate' and proportionate to the vast sums of money at stake. Up-front you'll pay the *brief fee*, then an agreed *'daily refresher'* for each day in court. If you are an equity partner in a top law firm, your earnings might compete with a top flight QC, but your total 'package', would need to be startlingly generous. And consistent.

A senior salaried partner in a good firm of solicitors can expect to be earning more than £200,000 p.a. whereas a busy junior barrister in the criminal courts relying on legal aid work can be on less than £25K. From that they pay their clerks a fee of usually 10% and often a contribution to chambers expenditure commonly on a rising scale according to one's year of call. A fair 'spectrum' for a reasonably successful junior salaried partner in a decent law firm would be somewhere between £85,000 p.a. to £120,000 p.a. So, the answer to the question is: there's plenty of money sloshing around. It's just a question of how bluffers get their hands on it.

In December 2018 the Bar Standards Board announced that as of 1 September 2019 the minimum pupillage award was to be £18,436 in London and £15,728 elsewhere. Those are the minimum figures (no account seems to be taken of whether the pupil earns anything in the second six-month period of pupillage) and will be considerably more for an exclusive high-powered set where parents are known to place their would-be legal wizard on the waiting list at *five years of age*); an average training contract for solicitors is now about £20K (slightly more for London, slightly less for outside) but much larger contracts are routinely offered by prestigious firms. At the beginning of 2019, the Law Society was recommending, as a matter of good practice, that providers of training contracts should pay their trainees £22,121 in London and £19,619 outside London. High-powered commercial firms offer a great deal more. Your best bet to get to the very top of the legal ladder is to start with stable, successful and ambitious blue-blooded parents, a private education and a 1st from Oxbridge; that is the case now and has been the case for over five hundred years. This fact of life may be unpalatable to some but should not deter the bluffer from joining the race; it is simply about understanding the odds involved.

By the way, the next time you bump into Her Majesty the Queen (as bluffers invariably do) ask her the following question:

Your Majesty. Having come to the throne in 1953 you have bestowed your wisdom upon fourteen Prime Ministers at the last count. Of those fourteen, how many did not go to Eton, Harrow or Oxbridge?

The answer of course is: two (Jim Callaghan and John Major). So, how do you get on when faced with the cruel bias of history if you are not fortunate enough to be on the right side of 'statistics' by the age of say eighteen? You must become a bluffer-in-law, that's how. Read on, because it is now necessary to focus upon the many varied ways in which you can practise the art of bluffing, make a decent living and retire gracefully at an age when you no longer need to sustain the bluff that you know more about law than you actually do.

BEING A LAWYER

In the noble art of bluffing, some background and history of your subject will invariably prove to be helpful. Especially on matters such as nomenclature – guaranteed to win valuable kudos if the subject comes up (which the bluffer will make sure of).

LAWYERS IN PERSPECTIVE

When Dick the butcher suggests to the rebel Jack Cade in William Shakespeare's Henry VI Part 2, *'The first thing we do, let's kill all the lawyers'*, he was referring to what we would now most easily recognise as barristers. It was not until the late 19th century, that the term 'lawyer' was commonly accepted to mean both solicitors and barristers.

By the time Charles Dickens published *Bleak House* in 1852, the term 'solicitor' was in common use, as was the term 'attorney-at-law'. Understanding these terms is a matter of some importance to the bluffer because attorneys practised in the common law courts, solicitors in the Court of Chancery, which applied principles of 'equity' (*see* pages 93–94) in contrast to common law. As will be seen later, the distinction between common law and equity is fundamental to understanding English law and its adoption in many places around the world.

Times have moved on from the 19th century (a bit); solicitors and more importantly 'chartered legal executive lawyers' are now to be found in a magistrate's court, or the local county court, and in the Crown Court.

Dickensian attorneys-at-law were killed off with the passing of the Judicature Acts 1873–75 and were subsumed into the profession of solicitors. Although by then it would not be uncommon for 'attorneys' to call themselves solicitors because the latter were thought to be a cut above attorneys.

By the beginning of the post-Victorian era, English lawyers had become increasingly polarised between barristers and solicitors. The two strands of the profession tended to look and sound different provided observers were able to distinguish between the middle- and upper-middle classes. Times have moved on from the 19th century (a bit); solicitors and more importantly 'chartered legal executive lawyers' are now to be found in a magistrate's court, or the local county court, and in the Crown Court. The lesson for the bluffer-in-law is that there are many ways to practise as a 'lawyer'.

TEN WAYS TO PRACTISE AS A LAWYER

There are numerous ways to practise as a lawyer and the bluffer-in-law should know as many as possible – because the real challenge is not just to find the right way for you to practise, but the best way not to get found out. This constant anxiety is sometimes known as the 'imposter syndrome'.

IN-HOUSE LAWYER
Working for a company as their in-house lawyer can be extremely lucrative and rewarding. Because you are part of the company you feel connected to their highs and lows and can have a profound influence on policy. But it is imperative to apply a commercial understanding to every aspect of your job; you work for a company, and that company must be competitive and profitable to survive. And survival is not just about the company's success but your success in getting on with other people, particularly those higher up the food chain. The most important question for the bluffer working in industry is not: 'How much do I get paid', but 'To whom do I report?' The temperament of the boss tends to make a difference, so choose your boss carefully. Better still, start off as the only in-house lawyer in a small company; the responsibility is empowering. And the right company will be willing to employ the right person suitably qualified for their needs,

so all levels of lawyers are in with a shout, paralegals and law graduates included. So if bluffers-in-law, armed with a degree in philosophy find themselves working as an in-house paralegal, their business card may well state: 'In-house Lawyer' and who is to challenge that? The invisible line is overstepped by a reference to *qualified* lawyer, which implies completion of a course such as a solicitor, barrister or legal executive. But there is no regulatory body which specifically polices the description 'lawyer'. That's a fact, not a bluff.

AS A BARRISTER-AT-LAW

Here again are two worlds: 'tenants' and 'the others' generally known as 'squatters' (imagine being in Valhalla waiting for your visa application to be approved) who have completed their 'second six' but have yet to be 'taken on' as a member of chambers and are now in their 'third six' picking up scraps of work from the senior clerk (who can make or break careers by the quality of briefs he hands out). Surprisingly, among tenants there is no real difference between junior and senior counsel – you're either a cost-sharing tenant, a member of the club, or you are not. Even QCs tend to treat all fellow members of chambers the same, except when in 'peacock mode' talking loudly and generally strutting about drawing attention to themselves, usually when fresh from the field of battle. However, if you notice that one of the louder member of chambers is uncharacteristically quiet it is because they have just lost a case and will not resurface until all is forgotten. It's a sort of 'ego-hibernation' period. But practising from chambers, particularly a traditional set in one of the Inns of Court can be a pleasantly comfortable way to earn a living if your chambers have a niche and collegiate atmosphere. The sense of camaraderie at the Bar can be deeply and genuinely life-enhancing.

IN A FIRM OF SOLICITORS

Here the hierarchy is brutal. There are equity partners – they own the firm and they are demigods with frightening powers. Read some John Grisham (start with *The Firm*) or watch the legal drama series *Suits*, or better still a rerun of *Boston Legal*. Below the equity partners are the salaried partners, most of whom will be traditionally trained solicitors. There follows a big drop to the 'associates' of which there are many and might well include ambitious barristers, overseas lawyers, legal executives and licensed conveyancers, all of whom are in with a fighting chance of top-flight promotion.

SOLE PRACTITIONER

Many solicitors prefer to be their own boss and practise alone, effectively a one-man regulated firm. There are many advantages to this way of life; you work your own hours and don't need to grovel to a senior colleague who you secretly want to throttle, slowly. Of course, there is a price to be paid for your independence; the hours may be 24/7 one week and zero the next. One time-consuming case can throw your well-laid plans into disarray. The money may be great one month and mortgage-threatening the next. However, if you can find the right balance and learn how to manage your clients, the freedom of being your own boss is liberating and deeply rewarding. And you can bluff to your heart's content, with nobody to call you out (apart from your clients, who must never be underestimated).

Many solicitors prefer to be their own boss and practise alone, effectively a one-man regulated firm. There are many advantages to this way of life; you work your own hours and don't need to grovel to a senior colleague who you secretly want to throttle.

REGULATORY JOBS

This involves making the leap from poacher to gamekeeper. Instead of bemoaning the number of regulators and the excessive red tape, why not join them? They need bluffers – good bluffers to outwit the bad bluffers. It takes one to know one (don't say that in the interview, it is a 'truth never to be told'). If the hat fits, wear it. But do your homework, make sure your would-be employer is not the subject of a cost-cutting review otherwise you'll be made redundant before you know it. Regulatory bodies are always mindful of the 'great culling' in 2012 when 106 'quangos' were put to the wall in a £2.6bn cost-cutting exercise including the now extinct 'Legal Services Ombudsman'.

ACADEMIA

'Those who can, do, those who can't, teach.' You may think the late and great George Bernard Shaw was being a tad unfair by so commenting, and prefer the axiom by Aristotle: *'Those who know, do. Those who understand, teach.'* This is all vital material for bluffers to absorb, especially for those who choose the academic life. There lies ahead a very rewarding career as a lecturer or teacher, and the status of 'professor' has a universal cachet, particularly if you continue your education in law by studying for a masters or Ph.D. The pay is unlikely to be anywhere near as good as that enjoyed by a successful commercial lawyer (play the long game – think of the pension and holidays), but for many it's a way of life that is far more acceptable than the cut and thrust of courtroom theatrics or interminable droning around a boardroom table.

THE CIVIL SERVICE

Those who work in the civil service will tell you that the television series *Yes, Minister* and *Yes, Prime Minister* are close to the mark when viewed from the perspective of the dynamics between those *in power* and those *in control*. In the maelstrom of real governmental power, it is more like the TV satire *The Thick of It*. It does take a specific type to thrive in this world but thrive they do. The successful ones are incredibly smart, both intellectually and emotionally. The pension is to die for, but it is probably best not to mention that as a prime motivator when applying for a job. The interviewer knows that already.

The civil service is always on the look-out for those who can think straight and act with a degree of professionalism associated with lawyers. Hence it is fertile hunting ground for the bluffer-in-law with a token legal qualification who is willing to enter the civil service world particularly in the context of management. Health, schools, immigration, police, judicial system, agriculture, industry, armed forces, taxation, infrastructure, climate change, counter-terrorism and global economics all need managers, like lawns need fertiliser.

EMPLOYEES OF THE CROWN

The UK does not have a public defence infrastructure. There is no such beast – yet – called a 'public defender'. Those caught up in the criminal legal system, if they can get legal aid, are likely in the first instance to be represented by a very young member of the Bar. Said young member of the Bar will do their jolly best to 'get a result' but will be unlikely to find themselves representing the defendant later in his criminal career. By the time the criminal-in-law has graduated to serious drug dealing or become a high-powered digital fraudster, the young barrister who got them off might well be working for the Crown Prosecution Service as a public prosecutor, a respectable career path for any qualified solicitor or barrister. Some lawyers are born to be public prosecutors. They were the ones at school who smarmed their way to become prefects and whispered in the teacher's ear who was smoking in the loo at break-time. They know who they are.

THE VIRTUAL LAWYER

In 2016 the HMCTS (Her Majesty's Courts and Tribunal Service) announced a £1bn court reform project aiming to 'bring new technology and modern ways of working to the way justice is administered'. These reforms when fully implemented (now expected in 2023) will have far-reaching effects on litigants and their representatives.

It is worth keeping a close eye on the roll-out of these reforms because those most likely to benefit will be the bluffers-in-law who understand that knowledge of the law and its arcane procedures is rapidly giving way to 'on-line services' and an increasing use of technology at the expense of 'real' courts.

The opportunities for the bluffer-in-law are endless because the skills required to 'win' contested cases in the digitised future will turn not on traditional legal training but understanding the digital processes involved in 'getting a result'. The traditional lawyers will be exposed as hapless bluffers while the quiet paralegal who understood that the firm's IT clients wanted to work with someone who understood 'their' world will be able to say to his boss: 'Who's bluffing now?'

NICHE LAWYERS

A licensed conveyancer, a trademark or patent attorney, an immigration adviser, a costs lawyer, notary public and commissioner for oaths are perfectly entitled as a matter of fact and law to call themselves lawyers. They are niche experts, trained and qualified in legal matters. Whoever says they are not *lawyers*, simply does not understand the meaning or history of the word.

BE NOT JUST A LAWYER BUT A *SPECIALIST*

What the bluffer-in-law will find out in the real world is that to really get ahead one needs to appear to be a *specialist* – preferably with a glowing reputation for being said specialist. But how do you attain this status without the experience, and how do you gain the experience without the knowledge or training? A medic completes a five-year master's course in order to qualify as a doctor . . . but to be a surgeon – a *specialist* surgeon – takes many years of further post-graduation study, supervision and examination. In the case of lawyers, to be a legal specialist in a specific field of law – in, for example: 'intellectual property', 'charity', 'consumer', 'regulatory', 'banking compliance', 'internet', 'computer software', 'conflict of laws', European law, or 'family' is a much-prized skill and one which the successful bluffer-in-law should master without borrowing another king's ransom for a post-graduate degree.

Sod it, scrap the niceties and forget any idea of playing by the book: use every connection you have and embrace 'nepotism' to mean 'the hand that fate dealt you'.

There are several ways around the apparent impasse of 'no experience, no expertise; no expertise, no practice':

- Write a series of blogs or articles about your desired speciality; demonstrate your knowledge and your *passion* for the field;
- Provide your services for free on a 'pro-bono' basis; you'll soon gain expertise;
- Get in the door at the most junior level of a firm which practises your specialist area;
- Gain an internship as soon as you can (16 is not too early) with a company that relies on the specialism you are seeking develop;
- Attend events where you can network and meet people who have the skills you seek and talk to them; you'll be surprised how helpful most 'specialists' are with an honest approach;
- Sod it, scrap the niceties and forget any idea of playing by the book: use every connection you have and embrace 'nepotism' to mean 'the hand that fate dealt you'.

How the law is categorised at undergraduate level and how different it is to the real world of legal practice and earning the sort of fees commanded by 'specialists' will be considered later. This is where the bluffer-in-law should be taking an extra special interest.

'Oh judge! Your damn laws! The good people don't need them, and the bad people don't obey them.'

Ammon Hennacy (anarchist)

COURT IN THE ACT

To know how the system works, the bluffer-in-law will need to know how many types of courts there are and roughly what they do.

THE COURT SYSTEM

The first distinction to be made is between criminal and civil matters. The criminal courts start with the Magistrates' Court and the Juvenile Court (which deal with 'young offenders'), the Crown Court, the Court of Appeal and the Supreme Court, known until recently as the House of Lords.

There are very detailed and specific rules governing each court, not least the question of who may appear on behalf of the defendant or appellant, claimant or respondent; and what powers of sentencing the court has and the extent and grounds upon which they may overrule decisions of the courts below them.

With civil courts, which include the Family Court, the position appears tricky from the outset. The 'lower' civil court is the County Court, but some actions may only be brought before the High Court (sitting in the Royal Courts of Justice in the Strand), for example claims for over £350,000 and *most* types of injunctions. Bluffers should note: the use of the word 'most' is what lawyers call a 'loaded' term; it means the true story is complex.

Don't try and find a 'small claims court' – they don't exist; it is simply another name for small claims in the County Court and is becoming increasingly an on-line software exercise.

So, in a civil context, the court of 'first instance' (i.e. where the claim or application is first made) may be either the County Court or the High Court. Don't try to find a 'small claims court' – they don't exist; it is simply another name for small claims in the County Court and is becoming increasingly an on-line software exercise.

The High Court can therefore act as a court of appeal from the County Court or a court of 'first instance' and from the High Court an appeal is to the Court of Appeal, Civil or Criminal Division.

From the Court of Appeal – both criminal and civil – the next stop is the Supreme Court. One of the main sticking points of Brexit is whether the Supreme Court, does in fact rule 'supremely' over England and Wales or whether the Supreme Court may be overruled by the courts of the EU.

So far this should all be known by an inquisitive passerby who has visited the Royal Courts of Justice in the Strand and therefore has seen in action the High Court as a court of first instance, heard an appeal from a County Court or from a Crown Court and has therefore witnessed the High Court as a court of appeal.

The passerby may have also wandered from the Strand, past Chancery Lane, down Fleet Street, past the Temple, and found his/her way to the Old Bailey (aka the Central Criminal Court), which sits as a Crown Court dealing with major criminal cases, seen a bit of a jury trial and heard an appeal against a sentence from a Magistrates' Court. Therefore, the passerby will know the Crown Court is both a court of 'first instance' and a court of appeal.

On a return bus back down the Strand and into Whitehall, the passerby could hop off to see the Houses of Parliament. Crossing Parliament Square they can look into a building declaring itself to be 'the Supreme Court' formerly the Middlesex Guildhall. If they are fortunate enough to be granted access and hear a case in the Supreme Court the passerby at this stage will know more about the court system in England and Wales than most lawyers.

But you are not a passerby, you are a bluffer, and therefore your semblance of knowledge should be somewhat more extensive and authoritative than that of a passerby or, indeed, most lawyers.

What you need to know, which is not obvious from the textbooks but helpfully set out in a *Bluffer's Guide* is this: the Royal Courts of Justice is an incredibly complex building, not just in terms of its external and internal structure but the legal history it embraces.

If in doubt as to which Division is the most appropriate always go for the 'Queen's Bench'. This is the default position of most trainee barristers while they are still bluffers-in-law.

If you do happen to visit the Royal Courts of Justice, you will discover that there are three principal divisions of the High Court which hear different types of cases, as in: the Queen's Bench Division, Chancery Division and the Family Division. If in doubt as to which Division is the most appropriate always go for the 'Queen's Bench'. This is the default position of most trainee barristers while they are still bluffers-in-law.

So, your client tells you: 'My DNA results are just in. My 'mother' is my sister and my 'aunt' is my mother, no one is sure who my father is and I have ten half-siblings I've never met. I want to sue my aunt for emotional stress, existential angst and breach of contract. Which division of the High Court deals with that sort of thing? Chancery, Family or Queen's Bench?'

The bluffer-in-law is calm, ready for this one: *'Well, it depends* [thoughtful pause]. *On balance I'd go for QB – they can always refer it to Chancery down the line. Family's a bit tied up with Russian divorces I hear.'*

JUDGES

There are numerous types of judges. What matters is being able to distinguish between the following types: **Magistrates** are of two types: lay magistrates (**Justices of the Peace** or 'JPs') and 'real' judges, referred to now as **District Judges** (who used to be known as Stipendiaries). The latter are salaried professional lawyers who expect to be addressed as 'Sir' or 'Madam'; the expression 'Your Worships' is more appropriate when addressing JPs. Magistrates are the ones who deal with the nitty-gritty of every-day usually minor crimes. They tend to treat all lawyers before them as bluffers-in-law if only to annoy the barristers who think they are 'slumming it in the mags' because they can't wear their wigs 'downstairs'.

Magistrates are often colloquially and collectively known as 'the bench', and have a 'chair' who is the only one allowed to speak or ask questions of defendants or witnesses.

Criminal proceedings invariably start off in the Magistrates' Court and are of three types:

- offences that can only be dealt with in the Magistrates' Court (e.g. minor assaults);
- offences which are triable 'either way' usually at the election of the defendant (including most forms of theft);
- and those triable only 'on indictment' in the Crown Court (such as rape and murder).

Magistrates' powers of sentencing are limited to six months' jail for a single offence, twelve months in total, or a fine. It can be a shock to the defendant who has pleaded or been found guilty for the magistrate to refer the matter to the Crown Court for sentencing. In other words, they are saying: 'This offence is too serious for my limited powers. Go upstairs and get properly whacked.' It happens quite often, usually followed by the words: 'Bail refused.'

Now, if the matter comes before the Crown Court, the judge will be either a **Circuit Judge** or a **Recorder**, the latter considered a lesser judge often only employed on a part-time, stand-by basis. Both expect to be referred to as 'Your Honour' except if they are sitting at the Old Bailey in which case better use 'My Lord' or 'My Lady'.

For female High Court judges 'My Lady' or 'Your Ladyship' is the correct form. Try to avoid 'M'lady' as you'll sound like Parker talking to Lady Penelope in *Thunderbirds*.

The defendant may on limited and very specific grounds appeal against the verdict of a jury or the sentence of the Crown Court judge to the High Court. The court attire of a **High Court judge** is slightly fancier than the lower judges and this is to remind everyone that they are far more important than the lower judges and hence they are automatically ennobled, by law, to 'Sir' or 'Dame'. Under no circumstances call a High Court judge by the term 'Sir' – you can expect a severe rebuff as in *'You're not in a magistrate's court now'*. 'M'Lud' or 'Your Lordship' will do. For female High Court judges 'My Lady' or 'Your Ladyship' is the correct form. Try to avoid 'M'lady' as you'll sound like Parker talking to Lady Penelope in *Thunderbirds* and be called out as a possible bluffer-in-law. And don't even think about calling a female High Court judge 'Dame' in court. While in the High Court ask to be directed towards the 'Bear Garden'. However tempting, it is not a good idea to ask for the *Beer Garden* as you will be escorted from the premises unceremoniously by a couple of beefy court ushers.

If you ever find the Bear Garden, you will notice several rooms called 'chambers' and outside there will be number of 'claimants' and 'defendants' looking nervous and confused. Inside these chambers are a small number of '**Masters**' who are for all intents and purposes High Court judges, except that they are not, really. Their chambers are quite informal rooms not 'proper' courtrooms and proceedings can feel more like an awkward meeting with a headmaster than a judge. The Master will be issuing 'directions' and 'orders' prior to the case being heard (or 'interlocutory' matters) in front of a fully charged High Court judge.

Masters have extensive powers and the importance of hearings before a Master should never be underestimated. In some circumstances they may even hear the case itself. Here, inside the Bear Garden, the bluffer will probably have absolutely no idea what is going on. That's OK, because neither will anyone else. That's the idea and it has taken many years of snail-like evolution to arrive at its Kafkaesque state. It's like a tactical game of chess being played out prior to the 'real' game of chess. In due course, after a few years, you will not only be able to find the Bear Garden without getting lost but also have a better understanding of the games afoot. 'Litigants in person' can be seen coming out of Masters' chambers not knowing whether they have 'won' or 'lost'. That moment happens when the opposing counsel explains the effect of the 'costs order' that has just been made.

A High Court judge is the real deal. Their powers follow them around, as if they are wearing a magic cloak. The next time you are sitting next to a High Court judge in a cinema or the opera, or in the check-out queue in Waitrose, ask them for an injunction; they have every right to dispense one there and then. The bluffer should by now be getting the point that the legal system is built on historical layers of power and status.

Numbers are of great value to the bluffer-in-law. Facts by their nature are not lies and a smattering of statistics, well timed, can create a polished veneer of authority; well-timed unsolicited pedantry is a fine weapon for any bluffer.

There are now over 400 District Judges, around 21,500 'judicial office holders' (more commonly referred to as 'Justices of the Peace'), over 600 Circuit Judges, less than 100 High Court Judges and 37 Appeal Judges or more formally, '**Lord Justices of Appeal**' and '**Lady Justices of Appeal**' (split is 29:8 in favour of the Lords). Let's not forget the 15 '**Masters**' because though their number is small they are a critical part of the smooth functioning of the High Court. At the top of the legal tree are the **Lords of Appeal in Ordinary**. In 2018 there were 10, although there is legal room for 12. The 'ordinary' bit means they are paid a salary as opposed to ordinary members of the House of Lords who are not. **Justices of the Supreme Court** – as they are now formally known since late 2009 – sit in judgement on appeals from the Court of Appeal if the Court of Appeal itself or the Supreme Court grants leave to hear a case which concerns 'an arguable point of law of general public importance'. The Supreme Court also hears appeals from the Court of Appeal of Northern Ireland and the Court of Sessions in Scotland.

There are a few very specialist judges (e.g. **Coroners**, **Judge Advocates of a Courts Martial**) and Chairmen of legally established tribunals (e.g. Immigration, Employment, Mental Health Review Tribunals), all of whom are very much part of the judicial landscape in the UK.

Quick test: *If you can distinguish between a Lord Justice of Appeal and a Lord of Appeal in Ordinary; a Justice of the Peace and a District Judge, a Circuit Judge and Recorder, carry on – you are well on your way to becoming a fully-fledged bluffer.*

*'If you have ten thousand regulations
you destroy all respect for the law.'*

Winston Churchill

MEET THE REGULATORS

It is a mistake to think that the regulation of lawyers comes about because of a perceived need for the public to be protected from the shyster-in-law. Shysters are conmen, they pretend to be what they are not, and they are a stain on humanity. Bluffers-in-law are essentially good people and every practising lawyer started as one.

The point is this: regulation of lawyers comes about because the 'real' lawyers need to establish a legal framework which validates their identity and bestows upon them exclusive membership of a club – with its culture, institutions, rules, rites of passage – and fees.

Hence it was solicitors who formed a club in June 1825 which acquired its first Royal Charter in 1831 to gain not just Parliamentary recognition but the blessing of the Crown – to a 'club' entitled: '*The Society of Attorneys, Solicitors, Proctors and others not being Barristers, practising in the Courts of Law and Equity of the United Kingdom*'.

In 1903 the name was changed to the now familiar 'the Law Society'.

Being an English club rooted in the early 19th century it should come as no surprise that women were barred from joining it until 1922.

The Bar did not gain legal recognition of its own club until some years after solicitors. According to the official website of 'the General Council of the Bar':

> *Discipline over the Bar has, since the reign of His Majesty King Edward I, been the responsibility of the judges, in practice carried out by the benchers of the Inns but subject to the visitorial jurisdiction of the judges. The General Council of the Bar (Bar Council) was formed in 1894 to deal with matters of professional etiquette.*

The word 'etiquette' is included because it is presumed solicitors do not know of such matters, nor should they enquire because the enquiry itself would be a breach of etiquette.

Bluffers may be wondering why the above passage – which is really about the history of the Bar Council – is placed under the heading of 'Discipline'. The answer is rooted in the Bar's concept of itself as an honourable society, with a pedigree and history unrivalled anywhere in the world; the word 'etiquette' is included because it is presumed solicitors do not know of such matters, nor should they enquire because the enquiry itself would be a breach of etiquette. Nor will they mention the fact that the Edward to which they refer – Edward I – died in 1307, because the Bar presumes you know your (English) history.

The reason for this diversion is because it was only very recently – as detailed in the Legal Services Act of 2007 – that the law intervened to dispel the idea that these clubs were not really regulators (in the sense of promoting and protecting consumers) but were more like . . . clubs in the sense of being defined legally and socially by their membership (in addition to promoting and protecting *themselves*). The 2007 Act created something entirely new – a 'top level' regulator, the Legal Services Board (the 'LSB', as you know). But the creation of the LSB was only one aspect of the new regulatory system because the Law Society and the General Council of the Bar were required to have a distinct regulatory arm in addition to their licensing functions. So, practitioners now have the Solicitors Regulation Authority (SRA) and Bar Standards Board (BSB) governed ultimately by the LSB.

Therefore between 2006 and 2008, the fundamental structure of the regulation of lawyers jumped from two bodies: the Law Society and the General Council of the Bar, to five (adding SRA, BSB and the LSB).

But we're not done yet. There is yet another regulatory body created under the 2007 Act referred to as the Office of Legal Complaints (the 'OLC') whose job it is to create an 'ombudsman scheme' including the appointment of a Legal Ombudsman. Who better to answer the question 'What does the Legal Ombudsman do?' than the Law Society:

> *The Legal Ombudsman deals with all public complaints across the entire legal sector (not just solicitors). The emphasis of the Ombudsman is on speed and informality, with the goal of resolving complaints by agreement rather than a quasi-judicial process. If agreed resolution is not possible, one of the team of ombudsmen will make a decision. But that decision will not be based on legal precedent or regulation but on a judgement based on what is fair and reasonable in the circumstances of that case, as required by the Legal Services Act 2010.*

Perhaps the bluffer-in-law might now agree that the whole regulatory framework surrounding lawyers is ready for some serious culling.

'You know what – there are so many regulators around it's like a rugby match with as many officials as players – I'll just call myself a lawyer and see who comes after me.'

Who regulates 'the lawyer'?

Good question. Not solicitors or barristers or legal executives but *lawyers*. That is, the bluffer-in-law, as honest as the day is long – who says, *'You know what –*

there are so many regulators around it's like a rugby match with as many officials as players – I'll just call myself a lawyer and see who comes after me. I'm not calling myself a solicitor, nor barrister, I'm not a legal executive, nor a notary, I've no interest in the CMC, QLP, CPE, CLE, CLC, BPTC, CIPA or the CITMA. I've got a degree – did a bit of law, I know the law. Ergo, I'm a lawyer.'

This brings us back to the fundamental way lawyers are now regulated in the UK. It is not just about what you call yourself, but what *rights* you have, or don't have. The key concept is the idea of a 'reserved legal activity' which under the 2007 Act is defined to mean:

- the exercise of a right of audience;
- the conduct of litigation;
- reserved instrument activities;
- probate activities;
- notarial activities;
- the administration of oaths.

And the restrictions do not end there because there is a further category of 'legal activity' which means, in addition to reserved legal activities:

any other activity which consists of one or both of the following:
- the provision of legal advice or assistance in connection with the application of the law or with any form of resolution of legal disputes;
- the provision of representation in connection with any matter concerning the application of the law or any form of resolution of legal disputes.

The result is that if you call yourself a lawyer without being authorised to engage in a particular legal activity there is a real exposure to a complaint which could result in criminal proceedings under section 17 of the 2007 Act which states:

> *It is an offence for a person*
> *(a) wilfully to pretend to be entitled to carry on any activity which is a reserved legal activity when that person is not so entitled, or*
> *(b) with the intention of implying falsely that that person is so entitled, to take or use any name, title or description.*

These offences carry a custodial sentence so people holding themselves out to be 'lawyers' are warned: be careful of the description you give yourself and be aware of the potential consequences of providing services if they fall within the definition of a 'legal activity' under the 2007 Act.

The net result of the current regulatory position comes to this: if you call yourself something you are not or hold yourself out as having the right to do something that you cannot, you are heading for a heavy fall.

Here's a test for the bluffer-in-law: the House of Commons in late 2018 considered that will writing should not be classified as a regulated activity under the 2007 Act. Hence you do not need to be a lawyer to hold yourself out as a 'professional will writer' but being a will writer does not make you a lawyer. Arguably if a 'will writer' called themselves a lawyer they are falsely implying that they have unspecified qualifications which justify the use of the term 'lawyer' and therefore fall foul of the criminal provisions of the 2007 Act.

Your best bet is to join a legal 'club' with a recognised professional status, and then take full advantage of the activities that it allows you to undertake. For example, by becoming a barrister, solicitor, legal executive, licensed conveyancer, trademark or patent attorney you belong to a club (with rules), are recognised as a member of the legal fraternity, and may call yourself whatever your club acknowledges to be a valid description.

There are two ways of looking at this: one is to think like a QC and write a long ambiguous treatise on the subject; the other is to ask yourself: 'Is the description of "lawyer", in its specific context misleading, or not?' If in doubt, retreat into classic bluffer-speak and say 'Well, it depends, best to *err on the side of caution*.' And that is always good advice.

'I have never managed to lose my old conviction that travel narrows the mind.'

G.K. Chesterton

THE GLOBAL CONTEXT

GOVERNING LAW

One of the most successful and unsung exports of England is its legal system – not necessarily in definitive and absolute detail, but in the broader terms of what is known as the 'Common Law' – a body of unwritten laws based on 'precedent' established by binding judgments reached by courts rather than made by statutes. Also known as judge-made law or case law, it spread throughout the British Empire to its many colonies, most of which retained the Common Law system after gaining independence (including the United States).

English Common Law is the preferred legal system for most Commonwealth Countries (of which there are 53 with a combined population of around 2.3 billion – a third of the entire world) and it is a daily negotiating battle as to which jurisdiction *governs the laws* of an international agreement.

It is impossible to quantify with any precision the percentage or number of contracts governed exclusively by 'the law of England and Wales' because such matters – by their nature – are confidential to the parties. But you can bet your bottom dollar that the governing law of most contracts between commercial companies based in the UK and companies based outside the UK, the law of choice to be applied in the event of a dispute, will be 'the law of England and Wales'. Even with American-based companies it is not uncommon to win the battle of the governing law because 'the law of England and Wales' is one jurisdiction, the jurisdictions of the USA being fifty and the 'governing law' clause will reference a specific state (e.g. 'this agreement is governed by the laws of California'). And American lawyers – whether they practise in California, New York or Texas – seem to have a trust in and cultural understanding of English Law and are often persuaded to amend the governing law clause to 'England and Wales'.

There are many reasons for the popularity of English law in a global commercial context, not least because so many countries seem to understand the fundamental principles of English law – from 'tort' to 'equity' (*see* pages 92/93). Besides, irrespective of the geo-political status quo and the history between nations, the third most popular language spoken and understood globally is English (behind Mandarin Chinese and Spanish).

If viewed as a business marketing and selling a commodity known as justice, then the English legal system is doing rather well, all things considered. The Commercial Court which hears cases in the Rolls Buildings (around the corner from the Royal Courts of Justice in the Strand) has a waiting list of a few weeks if the hearing is expected to last between 30 minutes and half a day, a few months if the hearing will take a couple of days and over two years if the case is expected to last more than a month.

Justice in the UK is a multi-million-pound industry in a very competitive 'dispute resolution' market. Hence the appointment of High Court judges is a tightly controlled system to ensure that the quality of the judiciary is top-drawer. It's an extremely successful commercial strategy, of world-class stature. Bluffers should point this out at every available opportunity, because it means more work and thus more fee income.

SCOTLAND

Scots Law is often said to have more in common with Roman-Dutch law than English law. It is a law unto itself, and always has been; even the Act of Union between England and Scotland in 1707 accepted that their legal systems were and should remain distinct entities. English and Welsh bluffers need to know this and hint that they have an extensive understanding of the Scottish legal system.

In Scotland there are no magistrates or Crown Courts. There are Justices of the Peace and Sheriff Courts, but the 'High Court' is very much a Scottish affair which sits both in Glasgow and Edinburgh and is called 'the High Court of Justiciary'. Do not fall into the trap of thinking that the systems are similar in all but name, far from it.

Every jurisdiction sets out and enforces its own standards and regulatory requirements. Scotland is no exception. It has its solicitors and advocates as England and Wales have their solicitors and barristers. To qualify and practise in Scotland you must abide by the rules of the Faculty of Advocates or the Scottish Law Society. Just as a Scottish lawyer seeking to qualify and practise in England would need to do under the rules of the Law Society of England and Wales or the General Council of the Bar.

When seeking to answer the question as to why Scotland has 15 jury members, paragraph 7.3 of the report told it as it is: 'We do not know why criminal juries in Scotland have 15 members.'

To give an idea of some of the more visible differences in a legal context between England and Scotland: juries number 15 in Scotland, 12 in England. There was an extensive review of the jury system in Scotland in 2008 by the Scottish government entitled 'The Modern Scottish Jury in Criminal Trials'. It was the first review on the subject for over 30 years and the last on record. It was as brief as it was honest, a lesson to bluffers anywhere. ('Least said, soonest mended' as the adage has it.) When seeking to answer the question as to why Scotland has 15 jury members, paragraph 7.3 of the report told it as it is: **'We do not know why criminal juries in Scotland have 15 members.'**

The Scottish jury may return a verdict of 'Not Proven' instead of 'Guilty' or 'Not Guilty'. If a jury in England and Wales came back from their deliberations and said 'Not Proven' the judge would most likely say: 'Do you mean not proven to be guilty or not proven to be not guilty. If the former then not guilty, if the latter then not guilty.'

There are far fewer jury trials in Scotland than England because in Scottish criminal cases the prosecution decides whether to elect for a jury trial. Following the review in 2008, the *Scotsman* reported later in 2009 that the total number of jury trials in Scotland during 2007/8 was 3,234; in England and Wales in the same period the number was nearly 80,000. Even taking into account the considerable difference in respective populations, this is still a significant disparity. On the civil side those who commence a claim in Scotland are 'pursuers' rather than 'claimants.' Scots are far more straightforward in their communications than the English, hence you do not *claim* a debt, you *pursue* one.

NORTHERN IRELAND

Northern Ireland maintains its own court system and judiciary, but with the Supreme Court of the United Kingdom remaining the highest court of appeal. As one of three legal jurisdictions in the UK, it operates a common law system which combines legislation and precedents through case law – much like England and Wales.

The Law Society for Northern Ireland requires English- and Welsh-qualified solicitors simply to complete a form (with such supporting evidence as is requested) and pay a fee if they wish to practise in Northern Ireland. However, solicitors with similar ambitions who qualified in Scotland are required 'to take further examinations and complete a period of apprenticeship'. (Further evidence, if needed, that Scotland's legal system is wholly distinct from that of England and Wales.)

There are over 600 members of the Bar of Northern Ireland. In order to join this 'highly selective' club it is best to engage with their 'Institute of Professional Legal Studies' in Queen's University, Belfast. Expect a long haul, similar to the hoops and loops required to practise as barrister in England and Wales.

WALES

It is surprisingly common to hear the expression 'England and Wales' as in *'this agreement shall be governed by the laws of England and Wales'*. It is important to remember that the Law Society representing and governing solicitors in England is formally entitled 'the Law Society of England *and Wales.*' The English and the Welsh are far more bonded in law than the English and the Irish or the English and the Scots. Unlike Scotland and Northern Ireland there is no separate Law Society for Wales, although there have been repeated efforts to create one over the years. There are nearly 4,000 solicitors practising in Wales in 450 firms (including 16 alternative business structures), but perhaps most lawyers practising in Wales have come to the view that it is better to qualify as a solicitor with the right to practise in England and Wales rather than create a regulatory structure which could result in having to qualify additionally to practise in England. And, possibly, pay two sets of regulatory fees for a 'dual' practising certificate. The same considerations apply to barristers because the Bar Council represents 'barristers of England and Wales'. As recently as July 2016 a Plaid Cymru proposal for a wholly separate legal jurisdiction in Wales was heavily defeated in the House of Commons.

EUROPEAN LAW IN THE BREXIT AGE

The United Kingdom voted on 23 June 2016 to leave the European Union, a departure which has not been without its problems. Perhaps the idea was that the disengagement of the UK from the EU would be like detaching a stand-alone annexe from a crumbling old property. But the complexity of Brexit* seems to have taken everyone by surprise. It seems as if the arrangements between the UK and the EU have become so intertwined that the entire building needs to be dismantled and reconstructed, piece by piece.

The UK had a referendum on the issue of joining the EEC (the European Economic Community, forerunner to the European Union) in 1975 and voted a resounding 'yes', by 67.2%. Fast forward nearly 45 years and the

* See The Bluffer's Guide to Brexit.

THE BLUFFER'S GUIDE TO LAW

result of the next referendum on whether to leave or remain was a clear (51.9%) vote in favour of leaving, which – while not exactly 'resounding' – was nonetheless a clear majority.

> After the UK joined the EU the ongoing debate has been the extent to which EU laws are applicable in the UK. Post-Brexit the question, as all good bluffers will know, will be 'To what extent are the EU laws *not* applicable in the UK?'

In the meantime, between 1975 and 2016, the UK submitted to the higher jurisdiction of the EU to make laws which are directly or indirectly applicable to the UK, as in a 'regulation' or a 'directive'. Equally as important are the two courts which have the power to make judgments outside the UK that are applicable to and binding upon the UK courts: the European Court of Justice (ECJ) and European Court of Human Rights (ECHR).

The ECJ, which sits in Luxembourg, decides on matters of EU law, its interpretation and enforceability. There are in fact two courts: the Court of Justice and the General Court, a constituent court of the ECJ which hears actions taken against EU institutions by individuals and member states.

These courts should not be confused with the ECHR,

because you will end up in the wrong country for a start – the ECHR sits in Strasbourg in France and is mainly concerned with the Human Rights Act which came into effect after the Second World War.

After the UK joined the EU the ongoing debate has been the extent to which EU laws are applicable in the UK. Post-Brexit the question, as all good bluffers will know, will be 'To what extent are the EU laws *not* applicable in the UK?', turning the dynamics of EU/UK legal debate on its head.

This debate will continue for many years because whatever the UK Parliament decides will be scrutinised by the European Courts come what may, if anything comes at all. It is inevitable that technical arguments will rage throughout the UK courts and into the European system for a very long time indeed, if not forever. The bluffer-in-law knows by now that the answer to the trickiest of Brexit-related queries such as, 'Post-Brexit, will we be obliged to eat chlorinated chicken?'

Answer: *'It depends. Best err on the side of caution.'*

Keep out of Chancery. . . . it's being ground to bits in a slow mill; it's being roasted at a slow fire; it's being stung to death by single bees; it's being drowned by drops; it's going mad by grains.

Charles Dickens (Bleak House)

FOUNDATIONS OF LAW

Most law courses will include a module on the history and/or the philosophy of law (aka 'jurisprudence'). A true bluffer-in-law should have complete confidence in the noble art of legal debate and the issues arising from both. Imagine, if you will, leaning against the mantelpiece of a grand open fireplace in your stately pile, having a decent chin-wag with the local bishop. Matters of concern might include questions such as: 'Can law exist in a secular society?' Or, 'What is the primary difference between "law" and "justice"?' Or maybe: 'Was Charles I executed or murdered?' The idea is to be able to pontificate on matters of jurisprudence with complete confidence; the very essence of the graduated, fully-fledged bluffer. It can save the day if you ever come across a High Court judge who yearns for the type of chat he used to have over cigars in the smoking room of his London club, swilling a decent port. The game is not to know or even pretend to know any answers but a subtler, more nuanced exploration of knowing what questions would be of interest to the gentlemen and ladies of law. The right question indicates a keen and learned mind and the bluffer has done the job simply by opening a line of philosophical enquiry of a legal nature.

CASE LAW AND LEGISLATION

Most people would understand in a modern context the term 'law' to mean a statute, being an Act of Parliament expressed as legislation. However, every section of every Act is open to interpretation (hence the existence of lawyers and courts). So, when lawyers talk of 'the law' they mean both legislation and 'case' law.

Parliament makes laws which are interpreted and applied by the judges. The keen bluffer-in-law will know this although sometimes even judges forget. This fundamental principle gets a bit blurred by the time an Appeal Court sits in judgement because to apply the 'common law' is a matter of analysing cases, as decided by judges. It is a fine line indeed between applying the law and making the judgement reflect the 'right' result. Unfortunately, one lifetime is not enough to unravel that one.

Fundamentally, common law is the idea of a judgment of a superior court being binding on a lower court. This is where the student of English law realises that the task of 'studying the law' is worthy of Sisyphus or Hercules. If you spent the next fifty years studying twelve hours a day you would only read a fraction of all the decided cases in England and Wales, let alone the European courts.

The judgment in any given case may be long and

complex, making it very difficult for the non-lawyer to make heads or tails of the result other than who has won and who has lost. And judgments in the same case may differ, fundamentally.

The bluffer should take great comfort in the fact that since 1996, after the publication of 'The Woolf Report' the trend both in court and in the context of written legal documentation was to make the civil and criminal legal systems more comprehensible.

The best way to understand case law is to read as many cases as you can (a course which the bluffer-in-law is unlikely to find too appealing). Start with the judgments of the highest courts because they will 'review' the decisions of the courts below and explain where they erred in fact or law. The challenge, which takes a lifetime to master, is to identify the 'ratio decidendi' of a judgment – the legal principle that is being applied in one case which will be binding on all lower courts. The bluffer should take great comfort in the fact that since 1996, after the publication of 'The Woolf Report' the trend both in court and in the context of written legal documentation was to make the civil and criminal legal systems more comprehensible.

Suddenly the use of Latin in court was frowned upon, legal documents became almost readable and what might have been called 'legalese' in times past suddenly became 'old school' making way for 'plain English'. If challenged by some Latin chit-chat best not to bluff a response but simply say: *'My, you're so pre-Woolf.'* Then see who's left red-faced.

TORT

The law of tort is a fundamental component of any law course and is likely to be a key first-year undergraduate class or module. Tort is case-law based and therefore the bluffer-in-law needs to understand how to read, analyse and apply the legal principles of a previous case to present circumstances. This task seems to come naturally to some students and is forever elusive to others.

The first step with tort is to understand its etymology: tort is a word that derives from the Latin word *'tortum'* which means a *wrong*. In this context the wrong is something which is actionable under the common law in the civil courts. You should start with the idea that we owe a 'duty of care' to our 'neighbours'. Unsurprisingly lawyers have argued for many years about who precisely is your neighbour and the extent and scope of the 'duty of care' that they might be owed. Tort is the basis for claims of common law negligence and if proved will result in reasonably foreseeable damages. Damages are of several different types from 'nominal', to 'general', to 'special'. The key point to understand is that just because there has been 'wrong-doing' by a 'tortfeasor' that does not mean that the court will automatically award damages like some sort of fine. In cases of negligence the lengthy arguments in court are often not about 'liability' but about 'quantum'; otherwise known as the 'so what?' defence. If a left-handed successful, professional musician had an accident resulting in their left hand being amputated, that is one matter; if a right-handed lawyer lost his left hand, that is another.

Start with the idea that we owe a 'duty of care' to our 'neighbours'. Unsurprisingly lawyers have argued for many years about who precisely is your neighbour and the extent and scope of the 'duty of care' that they might be owed.

A useful bluffing point is that there are laws which are tort-based but have been adopted into legislation. Defamation law (primarily addressed in the admirably brief Defamation Act 2013) is often called a 'hybrid' law being based in tort but now expressed in an Act of Parliament.

EQUITY

It is an article of faith that the concept of equity is a golden seam that runs through English legal history – the champion of justice over law. If a legal system does not have a history of equity then it cannot by its nature be said to be English in origin. Take, for example, Scots Law, which is alien territory to the practising English lawyer, and arguably more alien than the laws of any one of the fifty States of the US. The English common law is traditionally traced back to the 12th century under the rule of Henry II. As the common law developed so did a parallel set of rules or laws which were based on 'equity' or fairness because the strict application of the law could result in a legal decision that was perfectly logical and sound as matter of strict law, but nonetheless 'unconscionable'. The King delegated these responsibilities to his Lord Chancellor who was the *'keeper of the King's conscience'* and under whom the rules of equity grew.

As time moved on, the distinction and applicability of law as opposed to equity became so complex that Parliament decided that wholescale reform was needed, resulting in the Judicature Acts of the late 19th century.

When faced with a particularly knotty (i.e. incomprehensible) 'point of law', the bluffer-in-law may confidently assert: *'Hmm, interesting. Fairly predictable outcome in law, less so in equity.'* And then make your excuses and leave, pronto.

There are a few principles of equity still in play today, the most important of which is the fundamental point that all equitable remedies (including injunctions) are *discretionary* and best requested after lunch and certainly not during a bad innings of the English cricket team. In any event, the bluffer-in-law need only remember that the most important aspect to a successful application for an equitable remedy in the High Court is *courtesy to the Bench.*

TRUSTS

The Law of Trusts is a good example of what seems important to teachers of law yet is relatively tangential to those who practise law in most industries. A lawyer acting for a commercial firm (i.e. a commercial lawyer) might go from one year to the next without the thought of *'trust law'* crossing their mind. But within this body of law are very important principles such as the concept of a 'fiduciary relationship' which is a duty one person owes to another in circumstances of trust.

The heart of this matter is where one person owns or controls something of value not for their own benefit but for the benefit of another, such as an executor of a will, the trustees of a pension fund, an investment banker, drug courier, etc.

THE TAXONOMY OF LAWS

The bluffer-in-law needs to grasp the difference between legal subjects as taught 'in school' as opposed to the legal knowledge acquired in the real world – of money, promotion, dismissal, malpractice and bluffing, among myriad other matters. This is about classification of law; or in bluffer speak, 'the taxonomy of laws', and how different legal disciplines correlate.

Take the law of inheritance. Prudent and lawful advice on inheritance tax will potentially avoid a great deal of money going to Her Majesty's Revenue & Customs instead of one's family, favoured charity or other beneficiaries. Such delicate matters are sometimes expressed as *'private client law'*, which is a global business requiring a knowledge of the law as it relates to *finance, investment, inheritance* and *trusts*.

But will you find a course on *'money law'* covering all these matters? No, probably not. You can find courses on *'Tax Law'* or more specifically *'Income Tax'* and *'Corporation Tax'* or even *'Investment Law'*. Often such courses will include modules on *'Trusts'* because as you may have heard, it is not uncommon to use *trust law* as a means of avoiding a hefty tax liability, as in *'I know it's my round but, sorry, all my spare cash is tied up in a Trust Fund in the Cayman Islands.'*

The lesson is to be wary of what legal subjects are on offer; they may sound very interesting and intellectually stimulating but if the bluffer-in-law has an eye on being paid a fair sum of money by a company or a legal firm then a commercial understanding of the wider taxonomy of law is critical because you want to know what the company values not what your course considered relevant to your studies And you won't find that in a classroom.

For example, you might come across a course in *'commercial law'* but there is really no such thing; there is the law that applies to specific areas of commerce, sometimes referred to as *'mercantile law'* or even *'business law'*. If your company is involved in the transportation of goods by sea then you'll need to know about *'maritime law' or 'shipping law'*; if the goods are shipped by air then *'aviation law'*. If by both and – as is likely – cross-border rail services and road freight, then you need to know how all the rules and regulations relate to each other across different jurisdictions and be well versed primarily in *'contract law'*, the concept of *'conflict of laws'* and the international treaties that address such matters as in *'international law'*. Similarly, with a course in *'media law'*. There is no media law as such, but there are the laws that apply to the media.* If you worked for a television company you are immediately concerned with issues of *'privacy'*, *'data protection'*, *'regulatory law'*, *'contempt of court'*, *'defamation'*, *'employment law'*, *'health and safety laws'* of all descriptions and *'insurance'* matters.

Take also *'company law'* – as expressed in the Companies Act 2006, which has 1,300 sections, in 47 Parts, with 16 Schedules. It is quite possible – at a junior level – that you will never have to worry about such matters because that's the company secretary's job (thankfully) and he or she will tell you how many days' notice needs to be given before the next Shareholders' Meeting, when the accounts must be signed off along with every other important nitty-gritty detail that really does matter.

If you work for an insurance company as their only in-house lawyer (good luck) you would be expected to know not only about *'insurance law'* but the details of the insurance policies (back to basics *'contract law'*) and the whole gamut of *'consumer law'*, which to a large extent has been driven by *'European Law'*.

Imagine also being instructed by an estate agency which operates not as a formally registered company but as a partnership between family members. Better get up

---

* See *The Bluffer's Guide to Journalism* for a comprehensive synopsis of the law as it relates to media matters.

to speed with *'partnership law'* and some knowledge of land law (meaning *'property law'*) would not go amiss. If the terms of the lease under which your company's premises operates are due for renewal (i.e. an increase of rent and 'service charges' is on the horizon) an immediate crash course in *'landlord and tenant law'* is on the agenda.

If you prefer to specialise in the still relevant *'ecclesiastical law'* you would probably find one of the few law firms that understand how to make a living out of *'canon law'* – an arcane and labyrinthine set of ordinances and regulations mainly of Catholic origin.

Maybe you are feeling somewhat guilty about the fact that you are now so knowledgeable about niche areas of law that perhaps a spell working for a charity is the next logical step. That will require a very detailed understanding of *'charity law'*, expressed to some extent in the most recent Charities Act of 2011 which has 358 sections, 19 Parts and 11 Schedules. But before you take time out to harness that particular beast bear in mind that many donations to your charity will come about through trusts and wills so that's also *'trust law'* and *'inheritance law'* on your list. If you prefer to specialise in the still relevant *'ecclesiastical law'* you would probably find one of the few law firms that understand how to make a living out of *'canon law'* – an arcane and labyrinthine set of ordinances and regulations mainly of Catholic origin.

How about working for a very modern and hip digital marketing outfit where anyone over thirty years of age is practically Jurassic. Apart from understanding *'intellectual property law'* – copyright, design rights, patents, rights in data for starters – you will quickly need to understand that copyright is an international matter i.e. *'international law'* (again) and the rules that decide which laws prevail in one jurisdiction or another – *'conflict of laws' (again)*. That's before you draft the agreement between yourself and the company wondering whether you are drafting a contract of service (i.e. an employment contract which gives you legal rights and protection as an employee) or a contract for services, being a contract which is designed to avoid the company being held responsible under the Employment Act of 1996.

You must therefore be pretty au fait with UK *'employment law'*, which will require one eye on *European* employment law protecting the rights of workers across the EU.

Many issues regarding the current dual-track approach are still unresolved post-Brexit, and it is one of the 'big issues' that both Remainers and Brexiteers are (still) going on about.

But by this stage the bluffer-in-law should feel relatively confident that they can get away with an air of expertise regarding any Brexit-related legal matter. The reason for this is the knowledge that no lawyer can ever join a company and be expected to know all the rules and regulations of UK law, EU-law-in-transition, in both legislative and case law, under common law and in equity. At least not from day one.

Instead the bluffer-in-law, having learned the art of disguising profound ignorance as deep wisdom, knows where to find the answers quickly. That does not mean having access 24/7 to Google alerts, but knowing the right questions to ask.

Do say: *'You have been clearly wronged, no doubt about it. Just need to double-check whether your best legal remedy is under statute, tort or contract. Might try a route in equity.'*
Don't say: *'Bastards. We'll have an injunction up their arse before lunch.'*

CORE SUBJECTS

CRIMINAL LAW

A crime is an offence against *the Crown* in the UK, hence criminal cases are expressed as 'R. v Peter Smith', the 'R' standing for Regina (in Latin) or the Queen (in English). In the USA criminal cases are expressed as '*The People* against Peter Smith' (remember that their constitution commences with the words '*We the People of the United States of America* . . .'). It is still common practice for Commonwealth countries to use 'R v. . . .' in criminal cases where 'R.' can mean 'Rex', 'Regina' or the Crown.

Most criminal cases commence in the Magistrates' Court and are resolved there. Criminal offences are either: triable only in the Magistrates' Court, triable 'either way' (i.e. in the Magistrates' Court or the Crown Court, at the defendant's election) or triable *only on indictment*. The very serious offences triable only on indictment will be referred or 'committed' without discretion, to the Crown Court. Additionally, it is not uncommon for a defendant to be committed to the

Crown Court for sentencing after a trial in the 'Mags', particularly when the defendant has naively taken the magistrate for a silly old codger. Learn the hard way.

The core principle of criminal liability is that a crime requires both a guilty mind and a guilty act, called respectively 'mens rea' and 'actus reus'. However, this principle has been considerably diluted over the years and there are now many offences of *strict liability* which require only an act to be committed; the state of mind of the offender being relevant (possibly) to lessen the sentence, called formally 'mitigation'.

Where the principle of mens rea has a real significance is in the context of serious cases involving theft or serious bodily harm. An act of theft requires a dishonest state of mind. If you leave a supermarket with an item left in your trolley by mistake no theft has taken place because you did not intend to steal. If your rucksack is bulging with a variety of high-price items you cannot afford, your defence of 'honest mistake' is unlikely to be taken seriously, particularly if at the self-checkout you've only paid for a single banana.

Bear in mind that an independent witness always has greater value than your best mate who swears blind *'He didn't mean it Your Honour, and if he did mean it, he wasn't there anyway.'*

Although criminal law is generally fairly straightforward, an element of complexity creeps in when it comes to the laws and rules concerning the admissibility of evidence. In this context, the bluffer should remember that there are two critical issues: the technical admissibility of the evidence and the value or weight of the evidence. And bear in mind that an independent witness always has greater value than your best mate who swears blind *'He didn't mean it Your Honour, and if he did mean it, he wasn't there anyway.'*

CONTRACT LAW

The idea of a binding agreement between two or more parties being enforceable by the courts of the land is common to most jurisdictions around the world. If the bluffer-in-law is in a cynical mood, then contract law may be defined as how to get out of an agreement you now regret and how to enforce an agreement that never took place.

In contract law there are basic principles which apply across the board. Over the years it has become increasingly complex and multi-faceted, but the key is to ensure that the following principles stick:

1. The parties must have legal competence or 'capacity'. That is, of the right age (18 in most cases) and be 'compos mentis' (of sound mind).
2. The parties must have intended for their agreement to be legally binding. This rules out most so-called contracts made between mates over a few beers,

especially if reinforced with a man hug. A high five has no legal consequence.

3. There must be what is known as *consideration* or a *'quid pro quo'*. The consideration must be more than token, but the idea is that a one-sided promise made by one party to another is not the basis of a contract; there needs to be something exchanged. Lawyers will spend many an hour researching the latest developments in what constitutes consideration knowing full well that to get out of a contract on the basis of a lack of it is very difficult. To get around the 'consideration' argument you create a deed as opposed to a 'mere' contract, the difference being that a deed has a specific legal function such as the appointment of a trustee or the transfer of land and requires strict adherence to specific rules governing its wording and formalities of signing. If a document is properly 'executed' as a deed there is no requirement to prove consideration.

4. The agreement may be required in law to be in writing, such as the sale of land, or the transfer of copyright from one party to another. But mostly contracts are in oral form without being 'formalised' as a written document. This is great news for lawyers because people have an inherent ability to disagree about what they agreed upon, hence the dispute frequently turns on an exhaustive analysis of the admissibility and quality of the evidence – and so the billing begins.

5. The court will imply terms into contracts but only if they are persuaded that the implied term was capable of being expressed clearly and would have

been agreed had the issue been raised at the time the contract was being negotiated and prior to the agreement being concluded. It is far more difficult than might be assumed to persuade a court that a term was implied. The judge has heard it all before and will ask wearily: *'Yes, yes the Bench does accept the concept of an implied term. The point is how would such a term have been expressed by your client at the time the contract was being concluded, exactly?'*

Contract is sometimes referred to as a *'private law'* and rightly so. The law will respect the terms of engagement between private individuals from a distance and with some respect. Provided the terms are for a lawful purpose, are clearly expressed and fair then the likelihood is that a court would enforce them.

However, if the contract is between a company and a consumer, the law will not enforce an unfair term against the consumer: *'An unfair term of a consumer contract is not binding on the consumer.'* (That's a quote from the Consumer Act 2015, section 62 (1) if you want to set out your stall as an expert in consumer law.)

LAND LAW / PROPERTY LAW

Land law is often used synonymously with *'property law'* but as the bluffer might have spotted, there are many forms of property which are not land. Ultimately, all land in the UK belongs to the Crown and what everybody else holds are specific rights and responsibilities – known as an 'estate' in the land, which is not the same as ownership. If you die 'bona vacantia' – without an heir – the Crown will inherit your estate because, effectively, it will revert to its original and ultimate owner. It happens all the time.

This is a very important principle for the bluffer to grasp otherwise land law will always remain a mystery. Think in terms of having, for all time (or, 'in perpetuity' as lawyers prefer to say), the ownership of a house, or what you would call the 'freehold'. Your rights are concerned with the land on which the property is built as much as the property itself. Hence you can – subject of course to acquiring the right permission from the right authorities – demolish the building and build another one serving a different purpose.

'Restrictive covenants' and 'easements' are like rare diseases, which are a delight to the specialist and a nightmare to the unprepared. The land you think you own 'outright' may have restrictions placed upon it such as 'to be used as a single dwelling only' or 'not for use as an abattoir'. Or many other more obscure uses. These restrictions upon the use of the property manifest themselves in a surprising number of ways and cannot be ignored. Note that a restrictive covenant may be an obligation to do something or a requirement not to do something. (Either way the property holder should be aware of it.)

A property may also be subject to any number of 'easements' (or a 'right of way') not just in the sense of 'reasonable access' but real, physical infrastructure such as water pipes, electrical connections, gas supplies or waste disposal (a necessary euphemism for something which is also described as 'effluent'). Disputes concerning such matters are best placed in the hands of a specialist as the bluffer-in-law will soon become aware that even experts are sometimes found wanting in such proceedings. The stakes can be so high that QCs in this field demand – and are paid – their weight in platinum to 'get a result'. Contested cases in the Lands Tribunal are no place for the bluffer. Land law has changed dramatically in recent times because most disputes over land boundaries can be solved by the Land Registry Office. The records they keep, and their precise title plans with red lines, will resolve most disputes. If not, then expect to be off to the Lands Tribunal for an adjudication. It is advisable to be well prepared for that one because, if you lose, then the next stop is the High Court, by which time you'll have spent a small fortune in legal and expert fees.

Land law is a thriving and profitable business not just for property developers but for the experts that follow in their wake: lawyers, planning specialists, architects, surveyors, interior designers, landscapers, builders and all the trades and craftsmen that contribute to a property being bought for £X and sold for £2X in as short a space of time as possible.

FAMILY LAW

The law has recognised for a long time that issues concerning children, particularly when warring adults are involved, requires special rules and sensitivities.

The courts have come a long way since the days of Henry VIII because the law now accepts that decapitation is not really the answer, and that married couples cannot – or should not – be forced to remain married if the marriage has broken down 'irretrievably'.

These issues are very broad and include such questions as: What constitutes a legal marriage? On what grounds may lawfully wedded couples unwed? Once unwed, what responsibilities do the now-divorced parties have to each other? Which party should have custody of the children? And how may access by one party be realistically and fairly determined by the courts?

The courts have come a long way since the days of Henry VIII because the law now accepts that decapitation is not really the answer, and that married couples cannot – or should not – be forced to remain married if the marriage has broken down 'irretrievably' on very specific grounds: adultery, unreasonable behaviour, desertion, separation and consent. It's best for the bluffer-in-law not to know too much detail at this stage because the government is reviewing the grounds, process and consequences of divorce following a consultation process which ended in late 2018. The principal recommendation being considered is the view that divorce law should be amended to focus less on grounds of 'fault' (which encourage conflict and acrimony from the beginning) and concentrate more on the consequences of the divorce, particularly for the children. It's a bit late for the Royal Family, or maybe not.

HUMAN RIGHTS AND FREEDOMS

In 1998, the Human Rights Act was passed into UK law. The Act incorporated the European Convention of Human Rights drafted in the aftermath of the Second World War, which was enforceable in the UK courts in the 1960s but only through the European Court of Human Rights.

It was a Labour Party manifesto promise in the 1997 election to adopt the Convention into UK law and thus allow its terms to be enforced by the UK courts without having to spend on average five years going to Strasbourg to do so.

The principles of the Human Rights Convention are expressed as freedoms and rights including freedom of expression, thought, conscience and religion and the right to respect for one's private and family life, home and correspondence.

Bluffers-in-law might venture to suggest that the Convention must have been drafted with lawyers in mind, because the inherent conflict between a 'freedom of expression' and the 'right to privacy' is a constant battle fought out (at great cost) between tabloid newspapers and libel lawyers.*

* See The Bluffer's Guide to Journalism for a wider exposition of this matter.

What is sometimes overlooked is that the Convention entitles an individual to a fair trial, which includes a presumption of innocence, and once charged with a criminal offence *'the right to defend himself in person or through legal assistance of his own choosing or, if he has not sufficient means to pay for legal assistance, to be given it free when the interests of justice so require'*.

The legislative source of legal aid for criminal cases is therefore the Human Rights Act, but it is important to keep an eye on the fact that the provisions do not relate to cases in the civil courts.

THE LITIGATION GAME

Litigation (the process of taking civil legal action) has always been expensive, unpredictable and lengthy. Debates have raged over the years as to how to solve the dilemma of a 'just' legal system which is affordable to all. No government has squared that circle, anywhere in the world. If they had, it would have been widely copied. The focus here is on the economic dynamics of litigation because understanding the financial realities of litigation is more important to the bluffer-in-law than legal niceties. Clients want to know the raw dollar of it all, not legal detail.

MONEY, MONEY, MONEY

The grant of legal aid for cases in a criminal context was addressed internationally under the Human Rights Convention following the Second World War. For cases in the civil courts it remains an entirely different matter. The idea that justice in the civil courts would be open to all required some extensive arithmetic. Access to justice requires people with knowledge and experience of the law – lawyers and judges – but they take a long time to be trained and are costly. Don't forget that judges tend to live a long time and expect a decent pension. A 'system of justice' comes at a high price.

Legal aid schemes were placed on a modern footing in 1949 with the aim of addressing the challenge of effective access to justice (in both criminal and civil actions), but over the years the matter of funding became increasingly burdensome. Successive governments realised that a great deal of backtracking was needed because pithy aspirations such as 'justice for all' are a nice idea but ultimately extremely expensive. As stated by Lord Beecham during a House of Lords debate on the 'reform' of legal aid in 2014:

> At one time affording access to justice to 80% of the population it [legal aid] has, of course, undergone many changes in the last 62 years. Currently around 36% of the population fall within the financial eligibility limits, both income and capital, for legal advice and assistance, or representation, in matters of civil law.

One recent idea, thought to appease all sides, was the policy that *substantial* up-front court fees should be paid into the court before an action is commenced. Go to the Royal Courts of Justice and ask for the 'fees office'. There you will see young legal assistants and paralegals patiently waiting in line to have their claim form stamped with 'fee paid' before returning to another queue to have the claim form accepted by the court. At the front of the fees' counter you will hear plaintive mutterings such as: *'How much? When did the fee increase?'* *'Hold on I need to make a call.'* *'Do I need to go to the back of the queue?'* *'Call this justice?!'*

It won't do the bluffer any harm to have a working knowledge of the 'cost of litigation'. There is a table of 'up-front' fees which increase on a sliding scale from £25 for an online claim of less than £300 to £10,000 for a paper form fee if the claim is more than £200,000.

A claim for £20,000 requires a court fee of £1,000. That is a prohibitive sum to most litigants who are already £20,000 worse off, and why they are taking legal action in the first place. The contradiction of the principle that access to justice must mean affordable access while simultaneously imposing heavy up-front costs came to a head in 2017 when the trade union body, UNISON, took the then Lord Chancellor (Bluffer-in-Chief at the time, Chris Grayling) all the way to the Supreme Court. And surprise, surprise the LC lost, hands down.

The bluffer-in-law knows the correct response in such circumstances: 'Litigation is a tricky business, lots of issues to be addressed. What's your budget?'

Lord Reed ruled that government fees for access to Employment Tribunals were unlawful and delivered a speech as if lecturing the Lord Chancellor on the basic principles of constitutional law.

The lesson for the bluffer-in-law is this: imagine a very angry would-be-litigant who demands that you *'Sue the bastards. Immediately!'* The old school lawyer is thinking 'angry client pays top dollar' and will carefully explain all the ins and out of litigation before the client realises the 'free' consultation exercise came and went with the first coffee and the bill has now reached four figures, without a single decision in sight.

The bluffer-in-law knows the correct response in such circumstances: *'Litigation is a tricky business, lots of issues to be addressed. What's your budget?'*

It is worth noting that something known as Alternative Dispute Resolution (ADR) is a thriving industry. From the plethora of ADR websites in competition with each other it is clear many a QC has already defected from private practice at the Bar to the more lucrative shores of international mediation.

NO WIN, NO FEE

The culture that has been created in the absence of a free-flowing legal aid fund is the 'no win, no fee' deal, known as a 'contingency fee' agreement (*see* Glossary). A litigation lawyer will assess your case on a commercial basis. If it seems from their experience that it is a worthwhile investment of their time – with a clear and identifiable profit at the end of the rainbow – then they might take your case on (but on their terms and conditions). So the future is bright, but to survive and thrive bluffers should be thinking now of the next step in the history of the law before their hard-earned status is buried into the sub-strata of history.

Now pause, and think of peace and reconciliation – otherwise known as mediation.

MEDIATION

In the context of survival of the fittest – or the smartest – it is worth noting that something known as Alternative Dispute Resolution (ADR) is a thriving industry. From the plethora of ADR websites in competition with each other it is clear many a QC has already defected from private practice at the Bar to the more lucrative shores of international mediation, particularly to Hong Kong and west coast America.

The litigant's bible is called '*The White Book*' because it has a white cover. It contains all the detailed rules, regulations and practice directions needed to bluff through a hearing at the County Court to the Supreme Court. There are nearly 90 'Parts', which practitioners refer to as CPRs – 'civil procedure rules'. If you are sitting quietly at the back of one of the many courts in the High Court (Civil Division) you might just notice counsel pause and pick up their White Book, ruffle methodically through its many pages and say something like: *'I am grateful to M'Lud for raising that point; I believe it's addressed in CPR rule 3 paragraph 4, thank you.'*

Once you notice the term 'CPR' you will hear it more often, because the judge is constantly seeking reassurance that whatever ruling is eventually made can be traced to a precise paragraph of a specific rule, otherwise the judgment is likely to be appealed against. Buried in the White Book under 'CPR r.11' is the following:

If proceedings are issued, the parties may be required by the court to provide evidence that ADR has been considered. A party's silence in response to an invitation to participate or a refusal to participate in ADR might be considered unreasonable by the court and could lead to the court ordering that party to pay additional court costs.

This provision is of great value to the bluffer-in-law because it is so studiously avoided by so many trigger-happy lawyers. Having paid a few moments' attention to such detail, any suggestion of litigation can be responded to with a confident: *'Litigation's a mug's game. Better off with ADR.'*

There is a widespread misconception that the 'winning' party in a civil case will be awarded its costs as in the maxim 'costs follow the event'. But if the court decides that one party has acted unreasonably – particularly if it has not taken reasonable steps to engage in a meaningful alternative to litigation prior to proceedings being issued, the court can – and often does

– make an order as it sees fit according to the merits of the case under CPR r.44.

This can result in a winning claimant being ordered to pay the other side's costs, thus creating a very ambiguous 'result', because the ultimate award may be less than the costs required to be paid to the other side.

Having paid a few moments' attention to such detail, any suggestion of litigation can be responded to with a confident: *'Litigation's a mug's game. Better off with ADR.'*

Lawyers have become very alert to the dreaded 'adverse costs order' and ostensibly at least will make pre-litigation friendly overtures suggesting that the parties meet or engage in some form of agreed alternative dispute process. It is now common for such ADR provisions to be incorporated into all forms of contracts.

The obligation of the parties to at least appear to have attempted an ADR route before (and even during) litigation has spawned a lively satellite industry creating numerous self-styled 'mediators'. However, given the gold rush towards mediation – which has gone on for over 20 years – there are now so many mediators in a thriving and very competitive market place that even retired High Court judges cannot be guaranteed a steady flow of 'high-quality' (i.e. well-paid) mediation work.

The lesson for the bluffer-in-law is this: mediation can be seen to be increasingly a specialist branch of litigation. Reputation is the key to success, even more so than a competitive pricing policy. The usual business model is for the parties to share the costs of the mediator (who tend to charge on a sliding scale proportionate to the size of the claim). At the lower end of the scale £500 per day is not uncommon and the relatively modest mediator fees reflects the competitiveness in the market. On top of the fee for the mediator there will be other related costs such as the venue (and 'refreshments'). Unlike with most firms of lawyers, both solicitors' and barristers' mediation services tend to be very transparent and specific when detailing charges on their websites.

Mediation is often confused with meditation and arbitration. The former is often simply a typo and can be forgiven as such. Arbitration is a formal, statutory-based system of conflict resolution, which can be just as time consuming and expensive as litigation, though less predictable. Mediation, unlike arbitration, does not impose a binding resolution on the parties but seeks to find a constructive and consensual resolution to the dispute using the experience of a trained mediator. A successful mediator will work out how to resolve the dispute, not just on legal grounds but by applying a surprising degree of creativity and psychology to achieve a resolution in a single (albeit exhausting) day. For example, the resolution may involve one party agreeing to 'make good' the dispute in a manner that a court would find difficult to articulate and reluctant to enforce. But to the bluffer-in-law, mediation – in all its forms – can provide a very satisfying and rewarding way of making a decent living from helping to resolve disputes and not create them. There are many routes to making a living as a mediator, the law being just one of them.

If you've got this far and absorbed at least a modicum of the information and advice in these pages, you will now acknowledge that even the most experienced and overly qualified lawyer is and will always remain a *bluffer-in-law*.

The bluffer-in-law has accepted the indisputable fact that no one will ever know 'the law' because such a task is simply unfathomable. What is needed is confidence and fluency in bluffer-speak, hence the reason why this small tome will prove to be invaluable. So, the '*it depends*' response is arguably more helpful than '*I've no idea*'. The advice to '*err on the side of caution*' should be delivered with polished sincerity and weary experience. It is a truism that when considering litigation '*many factors have to be considered*' and that '*there is no merit throwing good money after bad*'. A wise response to any would-be litigant is always: '*What's your budget?*' because the point has been made, before going into detail, that such a course has a price tag on it.

Remember always that if your client decides to drive off a cliff (metaphorically speaking) the consequences were not your fault, because your advice – from the off – was '*Your chances of success are no more than 50/50.*' Excellent advice which says nothing at all.

GLOSSARY

Arbitration: a time-consuming and expensive alternative to time-consuming and expensive litigation.

Bencher: one who sits on the High Table in one of the four Inns of Court, not to be confused with a failed bluffer on a park bench with a can of Special Brew.

Bluffer-in-Chief: a legally unqualified Lord Chancellor.

Bluffer-in-law: an aspiring lawyer who others believe to be a 'qualified' lawyer due to their supreme confidence, self-belief and winning smile.

Capacity: the ability to challenge the barman for overcharging on the last round of shots.

Company Secretary: an undercover bluffer-in-law with great potential for a better job title.

Contingency Fee Arrangement: straightforward 'no win no fee' deal except as otherwise provided in the small print.

Counsel: a term used synonymously with barristers as in 'junior counsel'. 'Senior counsel' may mean a Queen's Counsel ('QC') or a polite term for an ageing barrister

THE BLUFFER'S GUIDE TO LAW

who, like Rumpole of the Bailey, has not and never will 'take silk' (the silk gown worn by QCs).

Equity: system of case law that developed outside common law case law which prevails over 'Law', according to some academic with historical issues.

European Union law: A body of law made somewhere across the English Channel known to cause severe existential angst to UK politicians.

House of Lords: the Upper Chamber of the Houses of Parliament, as opposed to the House of Commons (i.e. we *commoners*). Not to be confused with the Supreme Court or the Supremes.

Human rights: a default legal claim if no other claim of any substance exists.

Indictment: if 'charged' you phone a friend; if 'indicted' you phone a lawyer.

Inns of Court: the four Inns of Court around Chancery Lane in London: Gray's Inn, Lincoln's Inn, Middle Temple and Inner Temple. Middle does the best lunch, by far, and that's all the bluffer-in-law needs to know.

Lawyer: a term not defined under the Legal Services Act of 2007 because no one wants to regulate 'lawyers'.

Litigant in person: a 'LiP' or the 'bane of the judiciary'. It is a human right to defend oneself in a court of law, so they had it coming.

Lord Chief Justice: the Lord Chief Justice of England and Wales (LCJ) is the top dog in the judicial world. The LCJ is President of the Criminal Division of the Court of Appeal and Head of Criminal Justice, according to him.

McKenzie Friend: a bluffer-in-law who advises a litigant in person on a 'friendly' basis; treated as if invisible and inaudible by judges except in some family cases. Not to be confused with a shyster who has no friends.

Magistrate: the slogger of the criminal justice system in the Magistrates' Court who deals with people being 'out of order'. Being *well* out of order is dealt with in the Crown Court.

Master: a lesser known species of judge found in the Bear Garden of the High Court.

Not proven: a verdict acceptable from a jury in a criminal trial in Scotland meaning 'we tossed a coin and it landed sideways'.

Power of attorney: ancient legal right to cart a mother-in-law off to a home.

Probate: green light signalling deceased's money now available for that glamping holiday.

Proctor: a now redundant term for a lawyer who practised in the Ecclesiastical Court, historically appointed by the Archbishop of Canterbury and sadly missed by no one.

Pursuer: a Scotsman in pursuit of a debt.

Recorder: judicial term for circuit judge in their probationary period.

Supreme Court: according to Brexiteers the highest appellant court in the UK.

Taxonomy of law: the classification of legal subjects based in the real world, not academic modules.

Trustee: a jailhouse snitch often mistaken for a person in a position of trust looking after the interests of a beneficiary.

BLUFFER'S NOTES

124